When the Hekmats suffered

By

Dr Ameneh Sabzi Sarvestani

ISBN: 979889298784

To my beloved parents, whose existence is the light that illuminates my life,

and to all those who forever strive to elevate human knowledge and cultures.

Preface:

The biggest obstacle to the manifestation of the beauty of the human soul is "selfishness." Any factor that weakens human pride and selfishness will result in greater manifestation and display of the beauty of the soul.

One of these factors is "illness." It leads to the refinement and purification of the soul and cleanses it from existing evils. The difficulties and challenges of a person's life leave them perplexed and helpless until they also seek refuge in God Almighty and read His commands from the depths of their heart.

God, through illness, eliminates arrogance, selfishness, and vanity from humans, and during the inflictions, writes good deeds for them, just as they did in time of health.

Many benefits have been cited in narrations and scriptures for illness and pain for the sick individual, the best of which have been mentioned above. But the person who falls ill, unaware of this blessing, complains and is impatient, seeking immediate relief, but when they learn about its benefits, they endure and strive for spiritual ascent.

In verse 155 of Surah Baqarah, it is said, "We will certainly test you with fear, hunger, loss of wealth and lives, and diminished fruits, and give good tidings to the patient."

In one of the interpretations of Nahj al-Balagha, it is stated that God has placed pain and illness upon you as a means to eliminate your sins, as His decree is not rooted in illness but rather in the purging of sins, akin to leaves falling from trees. His retribution is only manifested through speech and actions (via the hands, feet, and body parts).

The chosen ones, whom God will welcome to heaven due to their genuine intentions and pure hearts, will enter paradise.

Philosophers and theologians have attempted to address the phenomenon of pain from different angles to shed light on some crucial questions.

One such question that has engaged the minds of philosophers and physicians in the past pertains to the cause of pain. Ibn Sina, both as a philosopher and a physician, has addressed the importance of the issue. Despite his adherence to the dominant views of his era, Ibn Sina does not exclusively attribute the cause of physical pain to the disconnection theory, but also acknowledges humoral imbalance as a contributing factor.

Sheikh al-Ra'is believes that empirical evidence is sufficient to prove the role of disconnection in causing pain. However, he resorts to reasoning to demonstrate the role of humoral imbalance.

Influenced by the natural sciences of his time, his theory faces challenges when confronted with counter-examples, leading to the conclusion that neither theory fully explains the cause of physical pain.

Descartes focused on the relationship between the mind and body. He believed that the mind and body are separate entities, allowing him to examine pain from two distinct perspectives. Descartes emphasized the importance of thinking and analyzing pain to better understand and manage it.

Aristotle believed that balancing the four elements (water, fire, earth, and air) is essential for physical and spiritual well-being, highlighting the importance of maintaining equilibrium in life.

These philosophers, each in their own way, have contributed to our understanding of pain and its management by examining it from different perspectives and providing insights that have become integral to modern medical practice and psychology.

Michel Foucault paid significant attention to the role of power and knowledge in the fields of medicine and health. Foucault highlighted how society and power systems can influence our understanding of illness and pain. He believed that medicine is not merely a science, but also a social construct that contributes to shaping perceptions of health and illness. In other words, pain and illness are not just individual experiences but are also influenced by social and cultural structures.

Foucault also explored the concept of illness as a social construct and emphasized that our understanding of pain and illness can be shaped by the power and knowledge within society. He delved into how individuals might be subjected to social and cultural pressures when dealing with pain and illness.

However, Friedrich Nietzsche particularly focused on the concepts of pain and suffering as part of human experience. Nietzsche believed that pain and suffering can serve as important factors in personal growth and transformation. He argued that hardships and challenges can help us become stronger and more independent. In other words, Nietzsche believed that pain can motivate us to seek meaning and purpose in life. He also referred to the notion of "will to power", which implies the human desire for growth, advancement, and overcoming challenges.

In this story, an attempt has been made to highlight the benefits and wisdom of pain and illness for the afflicted individual. By becoming aware of these insights, the individual suffering from disease can demonstrate greater resilience and endurance in facing difficulties and calamities.

It is hoped that with the recognition of the wisdom of pain, people will strive with patience and perseverance towards spiritual and existential growth, and appreciate the value of health and blessings that God has bestowed upon them.

With gratitude,

Ameneh Sabzi Sarvestani

1

With the help of her walking stick, the old lady moved from her ambush behind the window, to the front door entrance to catch the intruder as she enters the house from the yard.

“How did she get in? The old lady thought, “She must have the house keys. Who’s this woman, a thief? A woman thief— they steal in broad daylight these days?”

She stared angrily at the doorknob as the intruder turned it open and stepped in. It was a middle-aged woman, carrying a full nylon bag in her hand.

“Who the hell do you think you are, coming into my house like this?” the old lady yelled,” I’ve already called the police you know—“

“Mrs. Hekmat, it’s me, your nurse,” the woman answered calmly. She’d been told about the old lady’s condition, “I was hired by your son. He gave me the keys to your house.” She raised the nylon bag in her hand, “I did some shopping for you. If there is anything else you need, just let me know.'"

“Amir sent you? Are you his employee? Why did he send you? Why didn't he come himself? What’s your name? Where’s the other person? Why didn't they come?”

“My name’s Zahra, ma'am,” the nurse answered, trying not to laugh at the rapid interrogation, “I don't know who the previous person was or where they are now, but from now on, I’ll be at your service every day. Mr. Hekmat is busy with his business. He doesn’t have a lot of free time. If you need anything, come to me. Have you taken your medicine, dear?'"

"What business is it of yours about my medication? Why did you come here?"

"Whatever you need, I’ll do it. I’ll cook for you, clean and tidy the house—"

Zahra knew that if she kept at it, they’d be stuck in that back and forth till noon, so she put her stuff away in a corner and changed the subject, “What would you like for lunch, ma'am?”

"Anything is fine. I'm not ungrateful."

“Ma'am, is your son home?'" Zahra asked. She wanted to feel comfortable and take off her headscarf.

"Why do you want to know about him for? I don't know— I don’t think he came home last night. See if he’s in his room?"

Zahra preferred not to enter a young man’s room, so she assumed he wasn’t home just as the old lady said."

She picked up the shopping and went to the kitchen to clean it and prepare lunch. She took a quick look in the fridge, freezer, and cabinets, jotting down on a piece of paper the items she needed to buy next, then went to the old lady again to see if she needed to add anything else to the list.

"Have you taken your medicine, ma'am? Is there anything else you need me to bring you?"

“Did you say something?” asked the old lady, reclining on a two-seater sofa in the hall, listlessly staring at the picture of her late husband.

"Where are your pills? Mr. Hekmat said the instructions are on a piece of paper next to them."

"They’re on that niche over there. I took them. I can do that myself. They arrange them for me in their box so I can take them on time."

Zahra checked the daily compartmentalized pill box. It was empty. She arranged the pills back in their place then, glanced around the house. It was clean and tidy, so there was no need for sweeping or dusting.

The old lady and her young son, who was rarely home, were the only ones living there, so the house wouldn’t get messy very often. A maid also came to the house every day and took care of its condition.

"Ma'am, I'm going out to buy groceries. Is there anything I can get you?"

“I think we're out of fruit. You should buy a few kilograms."

"Yeah, I checked the fridge. I've noted it down, anything else?"

"No. Thank you."

Zahra returned to the kitchen and glanced at her watch. It was still too early to steam the rice. She checked on the pot on the stove, where the meat was slowly cooking.

She took the last few oranges in the fridge, made a juice and brought it to the old lady. She had to head for the supermarket around the corner. Mr. Hekmat had carefully described everything she needed to buy. He'd pay her for it later.

Her employer was a good man, kind-hearted and benevolent. Everyone knew the Hekmats as an esteemed and well-established family. They cared about other people. Everyone at work respected them. They were fair and paid everyone on time, not the type to steal, lie, or be deceitful. Unlike many in this day and age, who think being conniving is what you have to do to survive and not fall behind.

Zahra was new to the Hekmats' business, but that's what all the other employees said about them. Amir Company provided not only housekeeping services but also care for the elderly, children, and the sick. Their workload was heavy and they had a lot of customers. At times, there even was a shortage of workers.

For years, Zahra worked in the house of a wealthy, lonely old woman. When she died, one of her neighbors introduced Zahra to the Hekmats. Being part of a business earned her more money than working alone. She had to do that kind of work to maintain her dignity and keep her household afloat. Otherwise, like all women, she would've preferred to be a lady of her own house, instead of cleaning under other people's feet.

She had to manage life by herself. Her statue of a husband was an unemployed addict who couldn't even provide for his own use. Still, she preferred to keep the reputation of a married woman to preserve her honor and that of her daughters. She couldn't trust anyone. The world out there is full of wolves and pigs and a man in her life, even in that miserable condition, was a necessary compromise.

After finishing the shopping, she returned home with nylon bags full of fruit and dairy, took everything to the kitchen and started preparing lunch. She steamed the rice and let the Gheymeh[1] cook on the stove. While washing the fruit, the old lady's son suddenly appeared in the kitchen, eyes swollen red and hair disheveled.

Zahra quickly wore her headscarf. The boy opened the fridge to find something to eat. He didn't find what he was looking for, so he grabbed an apple from the sink, took a bite then went to examine the cooking on the stove.

"It'll be ready in half an hour," Zahra announced.

The boy put the lid back on the pot and went to the bathroom to wash up and comb his hair.

"Shahram, were you home?" the old lady asked uneasily, noticing her son's presence in the house, "When did you come home? You were out so late last night. Your car isn't in the yard— I didn't know you were here. "

"I came back early in the morning, parked the car out in the alley so I wouldn't wake you up. What's the problem?"

"Coming home so late—where do you go all night? Is this what you call a life? What about work? When are you going to pull yourself together and get married? Let me see you married while I'm still alive. Who's going to take care of you when I'm gone—"

"Oh, you're taking care of me are you? You're the one who needs taking care of. Don't worry about a wedding either, you'll see it when the time comes."

"You have someone in mind? Well, introduce her to us why don't you? Is she from a respectable family? Is she pretty?"

"Where did you get that idea? You're funny mom."

---

[1] An Iranian stew made of diced mutton, tomatoes, split peas and onion.

"Huh, I knew you didn't have it in you. How many times have I told you— let me arrange it with your cousin Ferdows. But you keep making excuses."

"Mom, how many times have I told you— that whining spoiled girl is no good for me. I swear to God, she's no good for me—"

He sighed, and went to his room. A few minutes later he was ready to leave the house, but he had to eat first. The food wasn't ready yet so he waited.

Zahra knew she shouldn't poke in family matters. She kept her head down, preparing the salad, but really did want to find out what the deal was with that old shrew. Eventually, her feminine curiosity got the better of her. She thought about how to start a conversation with the boy.

"When did your mother become so ill?" she asked.

"You mean her Alzheimer's?" the boy said, "It's been going on for a few years now. She had a mild stroke a couple of years before that. It's been downhill since then."

"Aw, poor thing, I pray for her health. Loneliness is such a terrible pain too. No matter what condition you have, it gets harder and more severe when you're alone. Wouldn't it be better for her well-being if she lived with your sister?"

"We don't have any sisters, just us three brothers."

"Haj Khanum2 doesn't have a daughter? What a shame, a daughter can take better care of her parents you know— especially her mother. She'd share her heartaches, keep her secrets.

---

[2] Literally means a Muslim woman who's done the Haj pilgrimage to Mecca. It's a common term to address elderly women in Iran.

"She could've had one, just didn't want to," Shahram said with a smirk.

"Why wouldn't she want one? All children are precious. It's not like there's a difference between a son and a daughter."

"She's not her own— my half-sister I mean. We have the same father, but her mom is my dad's first wife."

"What difference does it make? She's still a sister. Your mother could treat her like her own daughter. Does she live nearby? It would be nice if she visited once or twice a week."

"Not very far away, but she doesn't want to come here."

"Why not? How can someone not visit their family?"

"What do I Know? It has nothing to do with me. I keep my nose out of my elders' business. She's got a life of her own."

Shahram didn't have the patience for more questions, so he changed the subject, "Is the food ready yet? I have to go to work soon."

"Just a bit more."

Shahram got up and left the kitchen, throwing himself onto one of the living room couches. He turned on the TV and started watching the market channel. He did watch that one more than the others. The news was more relevant to him. For someone invested in the stock market, always being informed about trends and economic policies is a necessity. He spent most of his time home, doing that. He'd occasionally watch other channels as well.

He kept himself busy with TV for about half an hour, until Zahra told him food was ready. He asked her to serve it right there in the kitchen. He glanced at his mother. She was dozing off on the sofa.

"She'll wake up and eat when she's hungry," he thought.

Most of the day, the old lady was either asleep or dozing. Her medications had sedative effect. When she was awake, she quarreled with everyone, all the time. Her doctor believed it was because of the illness.

Taking care of their mother caused the children a lot of trouble. After the death of their father, she was always ill and had to see doctors all the time. The maids sent by Amir's company attended to her daily, helping with the household chores. Her two older sons were married, and had their own households to manage. Only Shahram remained home as a bachelor.

After having his meal he got up to head out. The old lady, just woken up from her nap, saw him leaving, "Where are you going now? Can't you stay home for a minute?"

"Stay home for what? I got work to do, life to live—"

"What life? I'll be gone soon, and you'll stay here, all alone with nobody to watch over you."

Shahram knew exactly what his mother meant, "So you want me to get married, so another woman can watch over what I do? What would I want that for?"

"You need someone to hold you together. Nobody knows when you come, go, or even where you are all the time!"

Shahram didn't have the patience to argue with his mother anymore, "I do whatever I want. It's my business, not yours."

He rushed out of the house, slamming the door behind him.

It was fascinating for Zahra to witness these arguments on her first day in that house. Every time the mother and son faced each other, they had some sort of dispute. It seemed that they were unable to coexist peacefully. Zahra was told that the elderly woman was ill-tempered, unintentionally rude, and a cynic because of her sickness, but in Zahra's opinion, all wealthy people were like that. She witnessed these quarrels in every household she worked in.

Another elderly woman she used to work for before was always arguing with her children as well. Looking at these people's lives from the outside, one would think they're in total peace and comfort, but when you get closer, all you see is frustration and distress, Zahra thought, comparing it to her own simple life. They didn't have much. They were just content with passing their days not being burdened by thoughts. There was nothing to fight over. Poverty left no room for arguments. All they needed was patience and effort.

She looked to the elderly woman slouching dejectedly on the sofa, "Haj Khanum, will you be having lunch now or later?" she asked, attempting to change her mood.

"It doesn't matter. Whenever is fine— did they announce the Adhan3 yet?"

"Yes, mam, just a few minutes ago."

"Alright, let me pray first, then bring me my meal."

"Sure mam. You need any help?"

"No, thank you."

---

[3] The Islamic call to prayer, broadcasted daily through television, radio and mosque speakers.

The old lady walked to the restroom to perform her ablution before prayer. Ever since she had a stroke, sitting on the ground had become difficult for her, and she couldn't pray that way, so Amir had bought her a special chair and placed it in the living room. She was firm in her belief to pray on time, no matter the circumstances.

Zahra preferred to serve the old lady's lunch and put her to bed quick, so she prepared her meal and brought it on a tray. Then placed it on the dining table, pulled out a chair, and waited for the old lady to finish her prayers. When she did, the old lady sat at the table. With Zahra's help, she had her lunch and noon medications with it. Then, Zahra helped her lie down for a nap in her room. She covered her with a blanket, and took the dirty dishes to the kitchen, where she ate her own meal. Afterward, she washed all the dishes, and put the leftovers in the refrigerator for the old lady's dinner.

She was supposed to stay there for eight hours a day. Since Shahram either didn't come home at night or returned very late, the old lady was alone most nights. Her being uncomfortable and annoyed by Shahram's absence was understandable. It's difficult for an elderly woman to cope with loneliness.

Leaving home, Shahram got into his car and drove off. Around that time of the day, he would usually meet with his friends in the main hall of the stock exchange, discussing prices and the status of various companies. This was his main occupation. He didn't have any other job. When he got his engineering degree, he searched for a decent job but couldn't find one. He wasn't interested in being a government employee either.

With the help of his friends, he invested a portion of the money he inherited from his father in the stock market. Initially, he didn't have a strong understanding of it, but after attending a few workshops, and benefiting from his friends' experience, he gradually got the hang of it. Although, he still wasn't as proficient as he aimed to be, he knew enough not to make costly mistakes. Occasionally, they would share their analysis with each other and achieved significant profit too.

The fact that the stock market still wasn't considered a reputable primary occupation in society bothered him. His family, especially his mother, didn't approve of his work conditions and almost regarded him unemployed.

He knew it would be better to have a job with a steady income and invest any extra money in the stock market. But, finding a suitable job proved to be challenging. He didn't like his main occupation to be stock trading, but he had no other choice at the time. He also had a house he'd rented out that provided a small income, but it wasn't enough to start a family. His mother and brothers constantly scolded him about that. But Shahram didn't like the girls around him. He thought they were shallow and only interested in money.

These girls accepted him as a suitor without hesitation. How could they not, a house, a white Persia4 and someone who provided for her somehow were the dream starter package for every girl out there. But none of them met Shahram's expectations. He didn't know how to find the girl of his dreams. He was looking for a woman who could stand on her own two feet, not someone dependent on a man's pocket. He wasn't attracted to the delicate, orange blossom-like, fragile girls. He sought someone he could trust, though he knew the chances of finding such a woman were slim.

---

[4] An Iranian facelift version of the French Peugeot 405, which is very popular among youth.

His mother was ill and couldn't go out and find him a suitable girl. His half-sister had cut ties with them after their father passed away, so he couldn't ask her either. She seemed to be living a good life. Shahram loved Nastaran like a true sister. Her husband was a university professor, and their two sons, Soroush and Saman, were medical students. She could probably find him someone in her social circle of her husband's family, but that wasn't an option after what happened.

Their eldest brother Masoud and their mother insisted that since Nastaran's mother had passed away, she had no right to their father's inheritance. Otherwise, Shahram and Amir weren't particularly concerned about the issue. Their mother argued that Nastaran was rude because she didn't show enough care and attention to her father during his illness, and that she didn't deserve any inheritance.

It wasn't like their father had left anything in her name anyway. All three of his sons owned properties in their names, but not Nastaran. Surely their father never intended to give her anything or else he could have done it himself when he was still alive. It's not uncommon for older generations to hesitate to leave anything to their daughters, as people say, "A daughter will marry, leave her family's home, and whatever she has will end up in her husband's family."

Shahram thought it was silly. Older women might've been content with that, but girls of this day and age didn't lose a penny to any man. That's why Nastaran had cut ties with them. She said that if she didn't have any rights in the family, then she wasn't a part of it anymore.

He arrived at the stock exchange building, parked his car in a corner, took his bag and went inside. Upon entering, he noticed his friends having a conversation. They were clearly upset. He greeted them and asked what the deal was?

"What should we bother going in?" said Arash with a scoff. "The market's crashed. All the charts are showing downward trends. The market's gone sentimental. These new sanctions have frightened everyone. People are selling out of fear. Whatever we do now, we lose money."

Ali shook his head in regret, "I say we should sell sooner. Let's save our capital— pull it out of the market. We'll lose more, the longer we wait."

Shahram paused for a moment, "It can't go on like this! No, it won't always remain this way. Eventually, these sanctions will be lifted, and the market will go back to its normal condition—"

"But this 'eventually' you're talking about could take years."

"Yeah, it could. That's why they say you should invest money you don't need right away in the stock market, so you could ignore it for a while if you had to."

"How long is this 'for a while'?"

"I don't know. I say we should just be patient for now. Let's do our analysis like always and keep an eye on the situation."

2

The doctor checked the old lady's blood pressure. It was fine. He conducted some neurological tests and compared them with her previous results, concluding that there was nothing unusual. He glanced at the test results and sighed, "All these Issues are related to her illness. She should continue taking her medications as before." He repeated his usual advice at the end.

Alzheimer's is a terrible burden for families. As parents age, it adds to their many problems. In the past, when the average lifespan was shorter, Alzheimer's wasn't as prevalent. It starts taking everything away from the patient one by one until eventually, it takes their life.

Amir was more attentive to their mother than the rest of his siblings. Everyone said daughters were more compassionate towards their parents, but this woman had none. She didn't want to herself. Probably never thought she'd be ill and alone one day. When people achieve a certain level of status and wealth, they barrel though life with an air of arrogance, but the faster they run, the harder their fall and eventual demise will be. They sink so deep that they can no longer rise.

Ever since her husband passed away, the old lady's troubles began. A couple of years later, her father died from a stroke. Then, Alzheimer's began eating at her, and loneliness made it worse. When women talk to each other and share their sorrows, they feel relieved and more resilient in dealing with problems. But, she left no one to confide in. Only Shahram was around and he was no shoulder to cry on. Nastaran had severed ties with everyone. The old lady did have a sister, but she was so preoccupied with life that she didn't have any time to take care of her sibling.

That left the old lady in an empty house full of problems. Masoud's childlessness also troubled her deeply. His wife, fearing someone might one day hint at a divorce, would bring up an argument and fight with her husband's family at every opportunity, to diverge from the real issue. Women's instigation of arguments usually serves a specific purpose. It's a strategy, a feminine ploy.

Amir, taking care of their mother more than his other two brothers, made life a little more bearable for her. He sent nurses from the company, took her to the doctor, got her medication, and drove her for tests.

He carefully held his mother by the hand. They took the elevator down. Her neurologist's office was on the fourth floor of an eight-story building filled with patients coming and going to various specialized doctors. Despite the many doctors in the city, there was no room to swing a cat in these clinics.

Most of these visits were because the doctors first ordered tests and follow-up visits. Eventually, a few pills were prescribed. This was repeated every few months. Their treatment methods were very similar to each other, but it wasn't possible to consider them inadequate. They were all graduates of the same school. Perhaps it was the fault of modern medicine. It's true that medical science's advanced by a lot compared to the past, but it also has its flaws and still can't cure many diseases.

Upon leaving the building, he helped his mother into the car and drove off. Caution was advised by the doctors. Because of her forgetfulness and occasional moments of distraction, they had to be careful she wouldn't end up alone in the house and not miss her medication. She needed assistance for all daily tasks, even her private ones. Osteoporosis5 added to her problems too. Amir would tell the nurses not to let her do any chores, lift heavy objects, fall, or be left alone even in the bathroom.

Through the entire ride, the old woman sat silently, leaning her head against the window. Amir locked the car doors so they wouldn't accidentally open. When her husband was alive, she was cheerful and sociable, played with her grandchildren and doted on her sons, but after the old man died, she got quieter and more withdrawn with each passing day. She seemed indifferent toward everything and spent her time sitting in a corner, lost in thought. The world no longer held any charm for her.

[5] An illness that causes bones to become weak and brittle.

There was nothing in it that interested her, perhaps because she had experienced everything her heart desired, and now lacked motivation for anything more.

It was nighttime when they arrived at the dark, silent house. The absence of Shahram was predictable and the nurse wasn't expected to be at the house during the nights. Most nights, the old lady was alone in the house.

She took her nightly pills and slept soundly until morning. Amir helped her out of the car, took her hand, and led her inside the house. He turned on one of the courtyard lights before they walk through it. He unlocked the entrance door and helped his mother enter.

Once she sat on the sofa, he checked the kitchen and refrigerator to make sure nothing was missing or damaged. He also examined the corners and rooms to see if his employee was performing her duties well. He verified his mother's pills. They weren't finished yet. He'd bring the ones the doctor had written later. He didn't have much time left. He had other errands to do, some shopping to do for his own home. He asked his mother if she needed anything, to which she indifferently shook her head. He said goodbye and left. On his way out, he turned off the courtyard light, knowing his mother neither had the patience to do it herself nor would she remember to.

3

Zahra unlocked the door and stepped inside to find the house a total mess. She hadn’t seen it like that since she began work there a week before. Women's clothing lay scattered among the rugs and pillows, even in the kitchen. She placed the groceries there, then went to check on the old lady. Unlike always, she wasn't on her recliner. Zahra looked around and spotted her sitting by in the bathroom, head buried in her hands. She greeted her and asked about her wellbeing, but the old lady didn't answer. Zahra sat beside her and kept asking questions, hoping to find out what was wrong. The old lady would shake her head indifferently, but as the questions persisted, she eventually broke down in tears.

Zahra kindly helped her get up and sit into her comfortable recliner. She handed her a paper towel and fetched a glass of water from the kitchen. Looked like the old lady hadn't taken her morning medication. She brought the pills and helped her take them with the water. That helped her relax, as she opened up to Zahra.

“You see, when you're young, everyone wants to be around you. But when you grow old, no one needs you anymore, and you're left alone with nothing to do."

"Oh don't say that Haj Khanum, God never leaves his worshipers alone. You have such wonderful children who care so much about you. You're our elder and we all respect you. We'll do anything for you. All you have to do is order. If you have any requests, please just let me know. I'm at your service. That's the whole reason why I'm here."

"It's no use. I forget even the smallest things. I can't remember anything."

"Dear mother, why don't you let me help you. You were looking for something, right?"

"I was searching for something, but I couldn't find it."

"Well, tell me what you're looking for, and I'll help you find it."

"It's nothing. I searched everywhere. Maybe I put it somewhere and forgot."

"It's alright. I'll find it for you. Can you tell me what it is and what it looks like?"

"It's a green silk scarf, the color is so soothing. Not one of those cheap, tacky ones. I looked everywhere but couldn't find it. It's vanished."

"Don't worry. I'll find it for you. If not, your closet is full of nice, classy outfits anyway— we'll buy you a new one that's even better."

"Nothing can be better than that one. I bought it at the Jeddah market when we went to Haj with my husband. I want that scarf only. Don't make promises you can't keep."

"I promise I'll find that same scarf for you. Now tell me, what would you like for lunch? I'll prepare it for you and then search for your scarf."

"I don't want lunch. I want my scarf. Don't try to trick me and buy one that looks like it. I want the exact same scarf, nothing else."

"Mam, I can't buy one like it because I haven't seen it before. I'll make sure to find the right one. I'll just have to do some chores ok? Now how about breakfast? Would you like me to bring you something?"

"No, I don't want anything. I only want my scarf."

Zahra knew the old lady hadn't eaten anything all morning. She went to the kitchen and arranged a slice of cheese, a few walnuts, and a sliced cucumber on a small plate and brought it along with a few pieces of bread. The old lady refused to eat first, but Zahra's gentle persuasion and careful feeding convinced her to eat a few bites with a glass of milk.

Once the old lady finished eating, Zahra took the dishes to the kitchen and started preparing lunch and cleaning up the plates. After she was done there, she began tidying up the house, picking up the clothes that were scattered everywhere. Meanwhile, the old lady snoozed on the couch, which allowed Zahra to work more comfortably.

Around noon, the old lady woke up. She opened her eyes and glanced around. The house was in good shape, and the aroma of food wafted in from the kitchen. It took only a few minutes for her to remember her missing scarf again. She looked around for Zahra, but couldn't see her. Feeling restless, she called out for her. Zahra was busy searching for the scarf and arranging clothes in the old lady's bedroom. She hurried out of the room came to her.

“Yes mam? Is everything alright? Do you need anything?"

"Where’ve you been? Where’s my scarf? Have you found it?"

"I've searched every corner of your room, but I can't find it. Do you remember where you last put it?"

"If I knew where it was, I wouldn't have asked you to find it!” The old lady retorted, visibly annoyed. “I wouldn't have bothered if I knew you were so useless. I don't understand why Amir sent you here in the first place— what's the point of having you around?"

That outburst upset Zahra but she reminded herself that the old lady’s bad temper and rudeness were because of her illness.

"I'll go look again, Haj Khanum. Don't worry. Just relax. Do you want me to bring you lunch?" She composed herself and said.

"You want to fool me like a child? You couldn't find it, and now you want to bring me lunch? Call Amir right now so I can get this over with."

That response offended Zahra. Having had enough of the old lady's toxic rant, she called her boss Amir and explained everything to him. Over the phone, Amir tried to calm her down and asked her to give the phone to her mother. After soothing his mother too, he promised to come as soon as possible to search for the scarf. He asked the old lady not to worry about it and focus only on her own well-being, telling her that stress and anxiety weren't good for her health.

The old lady tried to forget about the whole thing. She slowly got up and made her way to the bathroom, tapping on the floor with her walking stick. Zahra followed closely behind. She wasn't supposed to let her go to the bathroom alone. As the old lady entered the bathroom and began to take off her clothes, Zahra tried to help her but she resisted. Zahra couldn't leave the woman alone, even though her bad temper was hard to tolerate. Eventually, Zahra managed to help her remove her clothes. Then, led her inside the bathroom and sat her on the plastic stool, turned on the warm water.

She opened the shampoo bottle and tried to wash her hair, but the old lady shoved her away with a lot of screaming. Holding back tears, Zahra left the bathroom. If she had other options, if her husband wasn't an addict and had a decent job, she'd never have to endure such hardship and set foot in other people's homes as a maid. To make a living, she had to endure humiliation and mistreatment. If this old lady was bearable, her own children would live with her. She didn't have a daughter to take care of her, and a daughter-in-law would never. No matter what Zahra did for this old woman, she didn't appreciate it.

She wiped her tears. There was no other choice. She got up to wash her face when she heard a loud noise from the bathroom and then the old lady's scream. Her heart pounded with fear. "What do I tell Mr. Hekmat if something happens to his mother?"

She rushed into the steam filled bathroom. The old woman was lying on the bathroom floor, crying. She tried to help her stand up, but couldn't move from her spot. She turned off the shower and sat her on the bathroom bench, then left the door open and called her boss. She told him what happened asked him to contact an ambulance in case the old lady needed to be taken to the hospital.

4

They transferred the old lady to a private hospital. The emergency technicians themselves recommended it.

"Patients receive better care there in private hospitals," they said, "Government-funded hospitals are no good. Inexperienced medical students gamble with people's lives there."

Two nice young men lifted the old lady and placed her on a stretcher, otherwise, Zahra wouldn't have been able to manage that on her own. She could only turn off the shower, dress her in a warm outfit. The emergency services arrived in less than ten minutes. They entered the house, examined the old lady, took her blood pressure, and carefully lifted her onto a stretcher.

They assessed her level of consciousness and asked a few questions about the cause and manner of her accident. Then, covered her with a blanket and attached an IV to her hand. Zahra had to ride in the ambulance with her, but she didn't know where the insurance booklet, medical records, and previous test results were. Amir was better informed. She called him to find the insurance booklet, to which he said he was on his way and would soon reach the house to get it.

The ambulance was about to leave when Amir arrived. When he saw that her overall condition was good, he was somewhat relieved. The emergency technician explained to him that there was a possibility of a femur fracture and that it might need surgery. Amir knew how painful and problematic a femur fracture could be. He pondered, and then asked them to recommend the best orthopedic surgeon in town. The technician did so, but there was a problem—that surgeon only worked in a private hospital. He explained that they were responsible for transferring patients only to government hospitals, but Amir insisted that his mother should have surgery at the best private hospital in Shiraz. They promised him to make arrangements for this to happen.

The ambulance was about to depart. Amir asked Zahra to accompany his mother in the ambulance. He followed them in his own car. When they arrived at the government hospital's emergency room, a private ambulance was waiting for them. The technician had already spoken to them on the way. With their help, they quickly transferred the old lady from one ambulance to the other. They finally took the old lady to the private hospital, just as Amir wanted.

Everything proceeded smoothly at the private hospital's emergency room. They carefully lifted the patient from the stretcher and placed her on the bed. They brought their own clean blanket and gently placed it over her so she could stay warm. They even changed the old lady's wet clothes and took her blood pressure. While Amir filled the paperwork, they sent his mother for an X-ray. The radiologist confirmed the femur fracture. Amir was well aware of the hospital costs. But if they charge more, they provide better services he thought.

After the X-ray, they returned to the emergency room. A general practitioner examined the old lady from head to toe. He was a decent, good looking young man.

"Her only issue is the fracture, and she needs surgery," he said after the examination.

Amir insisted the specialist recommended by the emergency technician should examine and operate on his mother. The hospital's doctor agreed, saying that after performing the initial procedures on the patient, they would transfer her to the ward where their requested doctor would operate on her as soon as possible.

Amir's concerns slightly eased off, but he was worried about the costs. He decided to speak with the surgeon himself. The surgeon wasn't at the hospital then. Amir got the surgeon's office address from the nurses. They asked him to take the X-rays to the doctor's office and speak with him to learn about the treatment plan.

The nurses attended to the patient and completed her file. They removed the IV attached to her hand and replaced it with a new one. They drew some blood for testing and reserve, and then requested a detailed medical history, including any illnesses and medications she was taking. Zahra didn't have the precise information, but Amir had brought the medications she took to show them. When the nurses noticed aspirin among the prescriptions, they asked how long she'd been taking it.

"It's been a few years," Amir replied.

“The anesthesiologist needs to see her before the surgery, and the cardiologist should approve the operation,” they replied, “Regarding the medications she's taking, the specialists should give their opinions, but aspirin must be discontinued seven days prior to the surgery.

"How would a patient know seven days in advance that they're going to fall and break their leg?!" Amir asked anxiously.

"That's not what I meant sir. It's likely that they'll schedule the surgery for seven days later. It's not an emergency diagnosis, after all," The nurse replied.

"Well, it's an emergency for us. When will the surgery be scheduled?"

"First, the cardiologist and anesthesiologist need to examine her. If there are no issues, they'll determine the time of the surgery."

"Why do we need a cardiologist? My mother’s never had any heart problems."

"Well, she's elderly. This surgery can be quite demanding at her age. They need to assess her cardiac condition to prevent any possible complications during the operation."

Amir understood the nurse had a valid point, "So, when will the cardiologist come to examine her?"

“We've done our part. We’ll send her to the ward. They'll coordinate with the cardiologist and anesthesiologist. You’ll also need to talk to the attending physician to determine when the surgery can be scheduled. But she has to stop taking aspirin for now.

"Will there be any issues if she doesn't take aspirin?”

"I don't think so, but you can ask the cardiologist and anesthesiologist when you see them."

"Okay, thank you very much."

The nurse was right. These procedures had to be carried out. For an elderly patient with a history of several illnesses, it was crucial not to rush into surgery. It was better to consider all aspects and perform any necessary assessments.

The doctors' offices opened in the afternoon. Amir asked the nurse to give him the X-rays to show to the surgeon. Zahra's work shift was also coming to an end. Amir asked her to stay with his mother until Shahram arrives. He told her to stay while his mother was still at the hospital. Zahra did, she was his employee and had to listen to her boss.

Amir called Masoud and told him what happened. Masoud was his older brother and had to be aware of these family issues, although he rarely got involved.

Masoud had no children to be concerned about. His entire focus was on making money. He was in construction, buying apartment upon apartment, amassing wealth. Nobody knew what his purpose was in having so much money. Either way, he needed to know about their mother's situation, so that if something unfortunate were to happen, he wouldn't be able to play the role of a mourner. Masoud, feeling very upset, said that he'd be there as soon as possible.

Amir also needed to tell Shahram. The stock exchange closed in the afternoon, and he was likely with his friends at their family garden, as he was every day after work. All three brothers used that garden house, but it was mostly Shahram who spent time there.

He called Shahram, explained the situation to him and asked him to come to the hospital and stay with their mother until morning.

He could've asked his wife or Masoud's to stay with his mother overnight. It would've been more comfortable for her to have women by her side. But, neither Halleh nor Zhila were up for sleepless nights, nursing care, and staying at the hospital.

"For now, let's have Shahram stay one night and see how things go," he thought, "In the daytime, Zahra can come. And if she's unavailable, I'll send someone else from the company. I could send three shifts per day, but that would be too costly. Once she's discharged from the hospital, we'll need to arrange for a night nurse. I better start saving."

He hadn't told anyone at home, so he called his wife Halleh. It wasn't unusual for Amir to spend afternoons or evenings outside, so Halleh wasn't particularly worried about his absence. Often on Friday nights, Amir would get together out with his friends too. Halleh didn't particularly like her mother-in-law, but was saddened by the news.

Amir also called the company. Fortunately, everything seemed to be going smoothly. Of course, there were always dissatisfied customers, but helping people through their problems gave him a sense of fulfillment. He didn't have the patience to deal with overly demanding customers though. Some people had excessively high expectations, often anticipating much more than what they paid for. The employees he sent for services weren't flawless, but they managed to carry out their tasks, collect their payments, and leave.

Zahra was better than all of his other employees. She worked more diligently. Despite providing extensive training, guidance, and instructions to his staff, they still received complaints from customers. Both the customers asked for too much and the employees tended to be lazy. He was tired of this job and wished he could change it. There were some ideas in his mind but the right opportunity and circumstances hadn't arisen yet.

After reassuring Zahra that Shahram would be there soon, he took the X-rays and set off to the surgeon's office which was near the hospital. Upon arrival, several patients were waiting to see the doctor. He spoke with the receptionist, explaining that his mother was the surgeon's patient and had been admitted to the hospital. The receptionist asked him to wait until the doctor arrived. Amir sat in the waiting room for a few minutes until the doctor entered the office and proceeded directly to his room. Shortly after, the receptionist granted Amir permission to enter. Amir went inside, greeted the doctor, and introduced himself, "I'm Qamar Sepahi's son. The patient you admitted to the hospital today, she's my mother."

The doctor nodded. He took the images and contemplated for a moment. Perhaps he expected a call from the hospital informing him of the situation, but it didn't matter much to him that day. Sometimes, patients coming to the emergency room specifically requested his surgical services. The doctor asked why Amir's family requested him as their surgeon. Amir said it was the emergency technician's praise for the doctor. The doctor seemed delighted about it. He asked for the technician's name and details as he reviewed the images with a smile.

He pointed out the location of the fracture to Amir, "It's a hip neck fracture, requires prosthesis. The head needs complete replacement. And she has Osteoporosis I see."

"Yes, we've been aware of the bone condition for a while now. She's on medication, but where are we supposed to get this new prosthesis you mentioned?"

“Osteoporosis makes the surgery more complicated and time-consuming, but it's not necessarily a deal breaker. The surgery needs to be done. You don't have to worry about finding the prosthesis, the hospital staff will guide you through it.”

“I've been told that we also need to consult with a cardiologist and neurologist, and that the surgery would have to be delayed for a week because of the aspirin she was taking.”

“Why is she taking aspirin? Does she have a heart condition?”

“No, her doctor prescribed it after she had a stroke.”

“She had a stroke? What other medical conditions does she have?”

“She also has Alzheimer's disease— this Osteoporosis—that’s it.”

"Well, I pray for her healing, Insha'Allah[6]. It's better if she avoids aspirin for a week. We need to postpone her surgery for a few days to ensure the aspirin's effects wear off. Did she take it today as well?"

“I believe she did.”

“Alright, let’s wait a week for her own benefit. Aspirin is a blood thinner and can cause excessive bleeding during and after surgery. We need to be patient and let its effects fade.

“Ok, doctor. You know best."

---

[6] God willing

"You don't need to worry. I recommend she stays in the hospital this week. With this fracture, you won't be able to properly care for her at home. We'll keep an eye on her there, and we'll do everything necessary during this week to prepare her for the surgery. We'll perform thorough examinations to ensure she's ready for it."

"Thank you. I appreciate it. Doctor, I just wanted to ask about the costs—"

The doctor told Amir how much he needed to pay. Amir nodded, bid farewell and left the clinic."

5

In the morning, both the neurologist and cardiologist examined the old lady at the hospital. After reviewing her ECG and chest X-ray, the cardiologist approved the procedure and wrote instructions regarding anesthesia."

Zahra accompanied the old lady through the tests in the morning. She was impressed by the hospital's level of organization and the staff's professional behavior. The doctors said that the patient's sons needed to give consent for the surgery, so all three of them came and signed the papers, stating that they were aware of the risks. The surgery was scheduled for Wednesday of the following week.

Doctors always have a habit of making legal preparations in order to prevent any complications, even if the patient dies, their next of kin won't be able to sue anyone in particular except in case of a undisputed fatal mistake by the staff. There are legal remedies for cases where doctors have been negligent or made errors that caused harm to patients.

The three brothers finished their consultation. They booked a nice room, comfortable for their mother and the person staying overnight. A nurse had to be hired for the following nights. Their wives couldn't tolerate the hospital environment and the smell of disinfectants.

"How do some people work in a place like this?" they always complained, "It's unbearable. As soon as you enter, the smell of alcohol and disinfectants, Ugh— the air is filled with sickness and death. And the arguments with patients and their dissatisfied relatives— they're sick, of course they're agitated."

Amir went to the fridge to find something for the guests. His sisters-in-law were busy watching the television. They didn't have the habit of chatting much. Amir took out a box of pastries and offered some to them. He went to his mother first, but she tried not to eat much so she wouldn't need to use a bedpan. During the two days she'd been bedridden, she hadn't needed one.

Old age comes with all kinds of problems. First is loneliness. All the children are busy with their own lives and families. They don't always have the opportunity to spend time with their parents. Depression and isolation follow up, paving the way for even more illnesses. An old person can hardly handle all of that.

The old lady was no exception. Haj Hekmat had legally titled the house in his wife's name, making sure there'd be no disputes about inheritance after his death. He'd also deposited a sum of money in the bank, the interest of which covered her monthly expenses. Thanks to her late husband, she'd been comfortable without any serious problems, up until the sickness began.

The brothers discussed hospital expenses. There was the money for the surgery, hospital expenses and the nursing after they discharge her. In normal conditions, these weren't considered substantial for any of her sons individually, but each of them had his own headaches those days, and their capital stuck somewhere.

The exact amount of expenses was uncertain. They decided to pay the costs from their mother's own account until it wasn't possible anymore. Then, they'd divide the shortage among themselves. It was agreed that Amir would go home, find their mother's bankbook, check the balance and get her to sign it to withdraw money.

They told their mother. She agreed. She knew that although each of her boys went through some sort of financial issue, they wouldn't let her treatment be hindered by money.

A nurse entered the room, a sweet young lady. She greeted them, glanced with a smile and reminded them that visiting hours were over.

She gave the old lady an injection into her serum and two small pills to take orally. To maintain control over her condition, no one but the hospital staff was allowed her any medicine. They gave her the same pills for blood pressure, Alzheimer's, and Osteoporosis along with several painkillers and cough suppressants. Aspirin was off the table for the moment.

They had to leave soon. Zahra was gone, but the night nurse hadn't come yet. Amir scheduled two nursing shifts. Zahra would come in the morning and stay until the start of visiting hours. They'd be with the old lady during the two visiting hours. One of them would stay a few more hours until the night shift nurse arrives and she'd be there until morning. This way, they didn't need to hire three nurses and would save money.

They came to an arrangement. The night before, Shahram had stayed with her. That day, Masoud's wife, Zhila, was supposed to take over until the night nurse arrives. The others said goodbye and wished the old lady a speedy recovery.

6

The old lady emerged out of the operating room on a stretcher, covered in a blanket and an IV attached to her arm. She moaned in pain with drowsy eyes, as a man in a blue uniform pushed her. A nurse followed them holding her IV bag. An hour ago when the surgeon came out of the operating room, her sons asked him about their mother's condition. The doctor reassured them with a smile that the surgery was satisfactory and she could be discharged in a few days. “With all the money we’ve spent, it better be,” they thought.

Visiting hours had ended, but the children still waited outside the operating room. When they saw their mother on the stretcher, they all ran after her, asking the nurse about her condition. The nurse said that she was doing well.

“We’ll transfer her to her room.”

Everyone followed the stretcher down the hall and into the room. With the help of her sons, the care assistant lifted the sheets under her feet, elevated her, and gently placed her on her own bed. The nurse pulled up the bed's side rails, placed her IV on her, and pushed the stretcher out, closing the door behind her.

After the assistant left, a nurse came along, arranged the bed and installed a new IV on it. She pulled the urinary catheter from under the mattress and hung it at the foot of the bed, then measured the old lady's blood pressure and recorded it on the vital signs chart along with her pulse rate.

Amir, relieved at the operation's success, thanked the nurse. She acknowledged the gratitude with a smile before exiting the room.

The boys were satisfied upon seeing their mother's improved condition as well. They reassured themselves that going through the treatment troubles and covering the private hospital expenses were worth seeing their mother healthy again.

The doctor anticipated she'd soon be able to walk with a cane and some assistance. Although physical therapy was to be performed, everyone was well aware that her operated leg would never fully function like the other one. The family was content that she'd walk again, maybe perform personal tasks, and avoid being bedridden all the time.

Shahram was closest to his mother. He sat by her and held her hand, his eyes welling up with tears. He softly called out to her. The old lady opened her eyes for a moment, let out a groan then closed them again.

Masoud gently tapped his younger brother's shoulder, "Let her be. She hasn't fully regained consciousness yet. Let her rest."

Shahram got up and stood by the window, gazing absently at the hospital surroundings and the people moving about. Each person was there for a reason—some had an ailing mother, others a father, sister, spouse, child, or friend. There was some kind of bond.

He felt anxious about being alone, “If one day something happens to me for some reason— who’d take care of me?” He thought, “My mother’s already pretty sick. She won’t be around forever. There’s not much she can do in her condition anyway. My dad’s gone too. Sure, I have friends—brothers, but there’s still something missing in my life that only a soul mate could fill—someone I can share my sorrows and burdens with. I’m tired of being alone. I just can’t seem to find the right one.”

His gaze shifted to a few girls dressed in white coats. They were probably nurses. Doctors wouldn't have the time to stroll around like that. Private hospital nurses didn’t say very nice things about them. They said that doctors are too arrogant to mingle with.

Finding a suitable match weighed heavily on his mind, "My mother's surgeon was a middle-aged man— so I can’t find a single lady doctor? There has to be one out there. These doctors either marry late or never marry at all, and the divorce rates among them are high right? They seem to be living happily together, but they’re usually emotionally divorced— like a hidden divorce! Not all of them are like that of course, and some do have good lives together. But divorce is a real problem these days. They say one-third of marriages end in divorce, and many of those who don't divorce are just separated. My brothers are caught up in it too."

Witnessing his brothers' marital problems made him scared of marriage.

"Hey, you Ok? You’re staying tonight, right? We're about to leave."

Amir and Haleh had been at the hospital since morning. They wanted to see the old lady before the surgery and give her some encouragement. They'd only eaten sandwiches for lunch. The wait outside the operating room was too tiring. Mother was settled in the ward so there was no need for them to stay longer. They didn't want their kids to be alone. They'd returned from school by then and would mess up something soon if they were left unintended.

Haleh had made sandwiches for them and left them in the fridge for lunch. But she was still feeling uneasy. She wasn't used to leaving the children alone at home. Amir also couldn't leave the office unsupervised.

Masoud and Zhila also wanted to leave. They'd arrived later than Amir and Haleh. They didn't have children at home to worry about, but they were still exhausted. Reassured that Shahram would stay with their mother that night, they bid farewell to the old lady and wished her a good night's sleep. It was better for a man to stay with her on the first night after surgery to help her move around. They entrusted their mother to Shahram and left the ward.

Haleh and Amir headed home too. They were too exhausted to talk. Mental strain can be more tiring than physical fatigue. The car's movements lulled Haleh to sleep.

When they got off the car, their home seemed to be in order, no smell of burning or anything strange. Those little devils must have behaved. Haleh went to the kitchen and poured some water in the kettle. As she waited for it to boil for a cup of tea, her worries went away. Her concerns were just unfounded worries—mothers tend to have them. Whenever she came home a minute late, her heart would race with a thousand thoughts.

The children were quiet. They were playful kids and couldn't sit still for long. Haleh went to check on Delara first. She opened the door to her room. The girl was sitting quietly in a corner, doing her homework. She was in first grade. Haleh patted her gently on the head and asked if she'd eaten her lunch. She nodded and said they had their sandwiches together with her brother. A sweet innocent smile spread across her lips, the kind that could charm anyone.

Haleh felt at ease, but Dara was the older and more mischievous of the two. Boys are usually like that. He was a third grader. Their schools were close to each other, so they shared a school driver.

She opened Dara's room door. He wasn't there. She looked around. He was asleep on the couch with his toy cellphone in his hand. He loved that thing, it played music, and he loved to dance. He did since he was little. It wasn't typical for him to fall asleep on the couch in the afternoon. Maybe he'd been naughty at school. Haleh tried to pick him up to carry him to his bed, but he was too heavy. She called her husband and asked him to do it instead.

Amir came out of the bathroom, drying his hands. He was surprised to see his son sleeping on the couch too. They had difficulty getting him to sleep at night. He picked the boy up. As he lifted him, his head fell back, and his hands and feet drooped. He was completely limp. The parents exchanged a look of concern. Something didn't seem right. They placed the boy on the bed and called out to him, but he didn't respond. They called out louder and shook him, but there was still no response. Dara wasn't asleep—he was unconscious.

7

Amir and Haleh came back from the CT scan. Dara, as always, was restless and wouldn't stay still on the bed. No one understood why this healthy child, went unconscious the night before. All the tests from the emergency room turned out normal. To make sure, a brain CT scan was ordered. The radiologist performing the scan said everything appeared to be ordinary and there was nothing abnormal visible.

When they brought the boy to the emergency room, they washed out his stomach and gave him a glucose serum. Gradually, his condition improved, and his level of consciousness increased. By night, he fully recovered. His mischief began from that moment on.

The treating physician suggested that he might've consumed something poisonous like rat poison or pesticide, but they didn't have anything like that at home. Haleh never left any pills within the children's reach. Amir even went to check the house that night. Everything seemed in place, and the medicine packets appeared untouched in the refrigerator.

Haleh knew she had to go home and check things herself. She was more familiar with the house and had a better eye for detail, but Dara's condition at the hospital didn't allow her to leave for the moment. She'd left Delara with her father. In the pediatric ward, the mother had to stay with the child. It was easier to stick around when your own child is the patient. The nurses said if all the test results were normal, they'd discharge him in a day or two.

It was lunchtime, and since Dara's condition had improved, he was allowed to eat. A young man from the hospital kitchen brought their food in a tray. The food looked appetizing. Haleh, tasted a bite first, and it wasn't bad for hospital food. Dara ate it all eagerly. He hadn't eaten since the day before.

They were in the same hospital as the old lady, not in the same ward, though. The grandmother was in the fourth-floor surgical ward, while Dara was in the second-floor pediatric ward, but at least they were in the same place. They brought Dara there to avoid having to juggle between two different hospitals.

During visiting hours, the hospital was crowded. That day, the old lady received many visitors. Everyone who came to visit her learned about Dara's hospitalization and went down to visit him as well. Haleh asked Amir to bring some fruit and sweets when he came to the hospital so they could offer them to the visitors.

The pediatric ward was clean and well-organized, with brightly colored walls that set it apart from the others. Those were typically plain white, but this one had a more cheerful atmosphere. Drawings adorned the hallway and rooms, and playful plaster figures were affixed to doors. A playroom filled with toys was available too.

For Haleh, the experience of her child falling ill was a big challenge. Children were more vulnerable and less equipped to handle suffering, which made it harder for parents to witness. Mothers are willing to endure the illness themselves rather than see their children suffer.

Mothers burn up in the same fever, feel their child's pain and suffer the same ordeal. Eventually it's that love that creates most the foundation of life, and it grows in strength and glory every day.

Amir arrived before the visiting hours. He couldn't bear being away from his boy. The hospital staff was easy going on visitors. They were particularly understanding and would let more than one person in before visiting hours.

Seeing his son well and healthy, Amir's face beamed with joy. He was a parent who deeply cared for his children, willing to give her entire life for their well-being. When the doctor suggested that the boy might've ingested something toxic, the whole family turned the house upside down searching. They checked everything but found nothing—no empty medicine bottles or anything. They'd have to ask Dara himself. He was the only one who knew what happened. Amir glanced at his son. He was busy playing with his cellphone. He took his hands, "Son, do you remember yesterday, right before you fell asleep?"

Sensing what his father was about to ask, Dara nodded, his face contorting with discomfort, and regret.

"Do you remember what you ate? Did you have lunch with your sister?'

Dara looked at his father anxiously and nodded again.

"What did you have for lunch, dear?"

"The sandwiches Mom left in the fridge,"

"But did you eat something else later, sweetheart? Think hard, can you remember anything else?"

Dara paused for a moment, fearfully nodding in response. Haleh had previously tried questioning him in detail but hadn't figured out anything. She interrupted impatiently, "Let it go sweetheart. There's nothing for him to say. The doctors are probably mistaken. They can't figure anything out, so they blame the child. There was nothing in the house that he could've eaten. No! My children don't have the habit of eating just anything they find around. The doctors are mistaken."

"Yeah, you're probably right. I searched everywhere and didn't find anything either. You should take a look around when you go home, maybe you'll find something."

"There's nothing to find. I know my children well."

"Well, are they just making things up then. What about the CT scan? What did they say the results were?"

"It was a hassle. They kept saying he's going to move because he's a child, and that he'll need an anesthesiologist to put him under so he doesn't. We waited a long time for him to come."

"So what was the result?"

"They haven't given us the result yet. They said the radiologist has to review and report it, and they'll send the result to the ward by noon. But the guy who did the CT scan said it's good, there's nothing serious."

"Thank God. So they'll probably discharge him soon, right?"

"Yeah, the nurses say if the CT scan is good and he eats well, they'll discharge him. But we still don't know what caused it."

"So, he ate well?"

"Yes."

"Thank God. Maybe he ate something at school?"

"No, I asked him. He said he didn't eat anything at school except for the snack I packed for him."

"Alright then, God willing, it was nothing serious. I'll go check if the CT scan results are back."

8

Shahram wouldn’t leave his mother alone. He stayed with her every night. Zahra was there in the mornings, and at lunchtime, someone else took over. But at night he came himself, until morning. The emptiness of the house was hard for him to bear. He spent the days resting, visiting friends, and keeping track of the stock market. It wasn't in a good state. Trading was at a minimum. Everyone was cautious. They waited to see how the market would turn out. Professionals analyzed the situation and made trades in bad market conditions, but most of the others were inexperienced. They didn't know how to trade properly without loss. It’s not like every transaction is profitable.

There was too much on his plate. Seeing his mother lying in a hospital bed, he couldn't help but think about the possibility of not having her around for much longer.

"Life gets harder the older you get,” he thought, “You don’t get it when you’re a kid, head filled with childish games and mischief. As you age though, it starts to take its toll, preparing you to take on responsibilities. My mother's been through too much. She's worn out and past the point of no return. The surgery was to patch her up so she can be around for a few more years, manage her daily affairs hopefully. There's no way any of us could take care of her all day if she'd been bedridden for a long while."

The physiotherapist who came for her sessions couldn't do his job right because of the old lady's constant screaming. He didn't dare touch her. She was in a lot of pain after her surgery. She couldn't sleep the first night because of it. They gave her several morphine injections, but they didn't have much effect. Shahram was helpless, sitting on a chair by her. They gave her a ton of sleeping pills and sedatives, but none of them could put her to sleep.

She had to stay hospitalized for a few more days because of the prosthesis they'd implanted in place of her broken femoral head. It was the antibiotics administration that kept her in post-operative care. The physiotherapy could be done at home. It would take some time and consistent treatment for the pain to subside and for her to walk well again.

Zahra was very patient with her. She communicated gently. All those years of experience dealing with the elderly came in handy. She listened to their heartaches and didn't talk back much. She made sure the old lady was completely comfortable.

The old lady was already depressed, impatient, and irritable, but after the surgery, she closed off to others even more. No matter how much Zahra reached out to her with kindness, it didn't change her emotional condition. They didn't tell her about Dara's hospitalization. Zahra was also warned not to let anything slip from her mouth. The old lady was already dealing with enough pain and worry. They didn't want to get her more upset.

Haleh couldn't visit the day before. Amir told his mother that his wife wasn't feeling well. He made an excuse for his own lateness too. He bounced between the second and the fourth floor. There was work and home as well. Haleh had to stay with her son, so Amir was the one who had to care after Delara. In the mornings, Delara was at school, after that, she was either with her father or he'd leave her with his employees at the company.

Arash and Ali, Shahram's friends, came to visit him at the hospital along with their girlfriends. Shahram's girlfriend was with them too. They brought canned fruit, boxes of pastry, and a bouquet of flowers.

Shahram was used to drinking a lot of tea. He'd bring a flask when he stayed overnight. He'd get a headache if he didn't.

His girlfriend knew his habits, "We're having a tea party. Won't you join us?" she said teasingly.

"Don't you want an accompaniment with a tea flavor?"

He liked the jokes. In the hospital, he hooked up with one of the nurses. She didn't mind dating a rich guy. The private room was a clue to that. He wasn't bad-looking either. What could be better for a gold-digger than a good looking boy with money? In her head, it was just part of a game. It didn't matter how many other girls were after him. She only focused on what she wanted and ignored the rest.

It didn't matter to Shahram. All of those two faced girls, changing colors every day, were all the same to him. They brought no light to his life. The interest he showed in them was only to fill his loneliness and satisfy his instincts. Even though he pretended to be intimate with them, deep down, there was an emptiness within him that couldn't be filled.

He didn't need money for a house, or a company, and he wasn't interested in higher education. His engineering degree hadn't been very useful, so why would he want more of it? He wasn't keen on the idea of immigrating either. His friends who did live abroad weren't that happy.

"The grass is always greener on the other side," they said.

Something fundamental was missing from his life. If it were to be found, it would make everything else fall into place. It was the puzzle piece that would transform him. But he didn't know what it was or where to find it. No matter how much he searched, he came up empty-handed. Maybe he was looking in the wrong place. His thoughts were leading him nowhere and his destination remained a mystery.

He didn't pay much attention to religious obligations. He'd pray occasionally if he felt like it, and didn't have the patience for fasting either. He was mindful of halal and haram7 though.

Sitting on a prayer rug all day wasn't his thing. In his view, those who performed ablutions and prayed were just putting on a show to deceive people and exploit them. Too many times had he seen people in the bazaar pretending to be so devout and pious to trick people into trusting them. People who didn't know better thought they were the most righteous folks in the world. You'd mistake them for stage actors. It was all drama. His late father had a package full of bounced checks from that sort of guys.

Eventually, they never achieve anything. They all end up miserable and broke. Deceiving people never does work well. It always leads to failure and poverty, in this world and the next. Shahram's father didn't get what they owed him. They were left broke,

---

[7] The Islamic teaching that states; one must not take what does not belong to them.

unable to pay him back. They'd have to answer in the afterlife, the old man always said.

Witnessing that hypocrisy drove Shahram away from religious practice, although his faith remained steadfast. His values were rooted in his family upbringing. He was raised with good intentions and was charitable, always keeping his home open to those in need

His father had taught him the importance of doing good deeds. His brother Amir also practiced charity, as did his other brother Masoud. Their mother wasn't as active these days because of her health, but she used to be a pillar of support in charitable acts when her husband was alive. Shahram prayed for his mother's recovery sincerely and for his own success and happiness in life.

9

Amir had grown tired of his job for some time. He started "Amir Company" a couple of years back. In the beginning, when there were fewer customers, things were better. Employees worked more diligently and the customers were more satisfied. He'd started the company with the intention of getting married with the help of his father. He was young and had the patience and energy to deal with people, even the difficult ones. But now, he was tired of butting heads.

People became more demanding day by day. Not all of his employees were doing their jobs correctly. He knew that much. Some of them were dishonest, thieving, and lazy, but there was only so much he could control in terms of personnel. Supervising them all the time was impossible. He tried his best to select good ones and provided training and guidance as much as possible, but you can't change people's nature. Deep down, Amir understood the customers' frustration.

To be fair, they had some good customers too. They paid their fees on time, and treated the workers with respect, donated food, clothing, and household items employees in need. Amir believed that workers were the vulnerable members of society. You couldn't really blame them for their mistakes, and people in society were generally good and charitable with them.

He was well aware that just as demanding and overly expectant customers existed, so did negligent and cunning workers. That got him a couple of complaints every week. He managed to resolve most of them either through gentle persuasion, or by replacing the workers. A few times, he even recovered stolen items from the workers' homes and returned them to their owners. They took whatever they could, from kitchen utensils to jewelry, especially if it was a lonely, sick elderly person who couldn't keep an eye on their home. That's why he was very careful about who he sent where. The office staff had also been advised to be careful about where they sent which worker in his absence, but still, sometimes things slipped through.

On occasion, issues escalated to the point of formal complaints or lawsuits. All these constant headaches had worn him out. He no longer had the patience to deal with customers or employees.

He thought about starting a construction business like his brother Masoud, but that came with its own set of challenges. Dealing with laborers, architects, electricians, and all that, if he didn't oversee the work himself, no matter how he dealt with these people, they'd always try to take advantage somehow.

Shahram, on the other hand, had made life easier for himself with the stock market. It had its good and bad days though. Sometimes you profit, but there were losses too. Sometimes trade stops altogether because the market crashes. Amir couldn't figure it out anyway. He didn't have the patience to attend classes and workshops either. These jobs demand constant attention too. It's more suitable for young people.

The hand woven carpet business his late father ran was good as long as it was popular, but the market got so stagnant that the old man himself closed it down while he was still alive and abandoned it. He shut down the whole factory, sold all the machines at scrap metal prices. Years before, he'd imported all his machinery from abroad. Other provinces produced and used Iranian-made machines, but his father decided to listen to his partner in hope of better quality. They wanted to produce finer yarns and ultimately weave better carpets for export.

Amir himself, like his father, loved Iranian carpets and handicrafts very much. He considered it a part of their identity and culture. For centuries, the patterns of Iranian carpets have been rooted in their memories, culture, and art, but unfortunately, the economy wouldn’t allow rebuilding that business. When it was booming, their lives were vibrant. They were flush with cash, and life was good as gold. Their door was open and house bustling. They took care of other families too. The old man bought wool from farmers for spinning. Not every type of wool was suitable for those machines.

They spun the best type of wool and sold the yarn to dyers. After dyeing, it was sent to women who mostly wove carpets at home. Most women weavers only received the weaving fee, and the woven carpet was handed over to the same employer that provided them with the yarn. Many families' lives made a living through this cycle, from the shepherd who sold the wool of his grazing sheep to the old woman who spun yarn in the corner of her house. From everyday workers with minimal literacy and financial means to wholesalers and carpet exporters, all benefited from that abundance. All their lives were adorned with the colored pattern of the carpets.

Every time Amir remembered the carpet business days he’d feel sad. Hand woven carpets weren’t made like they used to be. His father was convinced that it was a dead-end job. Amateurs who didn’t know anything about the industry started trading bad checks. They’d gable it all, unable to pay back people's loans, causing trouble for everyone else. Those idiots ruined the market.

His father grew tired and gave it up eventually. Many of his colleagues did the same. Some older folks went bankrupt and died out of shame. If the carpet business still had its former glory, he himself, as well as Masoud and Shahram, wouldn't have had to look for other work. All three of them could continue doing their family business. They sure had the background experience for it, and their father's reputation in the market was more valuable than anything else. They wouldn't as dissatisfied as they were then.

Their father didn't have formal education himself, but he encouraged his children to continue theirs. All of them went to university and got degrees in different fields. Their degrees didn't have any impact on their careers though.

Higher education affects personally in a way that can influence someone for the rest of their life. But when education and work are in the same context, it's much more beneficial for society as a whole.

It doesn't make sense for someone with a mining degree to start a housekeeping and elderly care company, or for an unemployed materials engineering graduate to do construction, or In Shahram's case, an agricultural engineer to dedicate his precious time to the unrelenting fluctuation of the stock market. This inconsistency is visible in every part of Iran, from education to the economy.

True that the carpet market was down, but Iran's handicraft industries are not limited to carpets. There are a lot of crafts that belong to Iranians only. If the government paid attention to them, they can provide just as much commendable work and income, and keep the wheel of people's lives turning. When poverty, unemployment, and hunger take root, corruption and embezzlement follow. A person with a full stomach won't resort to theft, corruption, or fraud.

Amir's mind was exhausted, jumping from one subject to another, like an ape, roaming anywhere and everywhere, disturbing the peace. Nothing is more important than peace of mind, he thought. When he didn't have it, managing life and work slipped out of his hands.

He sometimes felt bad that he wasn't reaching the spiritual depth within himself. He wasn't giving enough attention to religious matters and felt a sense of guilt about it. That lifestyle was far from what he thought it should be, but perhaps he'd gotten used to it, or maybe lacked the willpower to change it. He needed an inner effort. People always say, "It's up to us." Years had passed in pursuit of pleasure, and this desire for comfort had weakened his will and drained his energy. Mother's condition was an untimely addition to all the struggles.

The whole family's luck had gotten rotten. His father's job, his own, and his brothers' didn't get them anywhere. The Iranian rug was the pinnacle of craft and wealth one day, now gone down the drain. It seemed that society was falling behind day by day, growing more distant from the rest of the world. Nothing was in its place. People weren't in their right state of mind and didn't have the nerves for anything anymore.

Everyone was caught up in competition with one another, struggling to put food on the table, and none were satisfied. Perhaps it was haram8 money that intoxicated people's minds. Or maybe it wasn't the financial issue that came up, but rather the way they obtained it that satisfied their sense of vanity and inner egos. Obtaining something along with the corruption of others gave them a greater sense of identity than when they just made money through hard work. There are some, the work of whom benefits both themselves and others. With constructiveness, they build their own world and their afterlife. But people like that are rare.

There are few with ties to big players in the government who could move forward without any problems, eventually being

---

8 Ill-gotten wealth obtained through sin.

called entrepreneurs. Amir didn't want to work for anyone else, but there was no place for people like him in the country. He wasn't connected, nor was he one for bribery, theft, or freeloading. He just wanted to mind his own business, which only brought him frustration. How couldn't take it anymore. After that, headaches like that make you age faster and fall sick more often. If only he could leave for good.

His cousin in Toronto always praised the social culture there. He'd say it's worth working all day. It's difficult at first for a newcomer, but after a while, work and life fall into place. It would be better for his children's future if they grew up there. His cousin lived a bachelor's life there, less trouble than a man with a wife and two kids that way.

He stayed there for a few years before obtaining his residency. Now, no matter how much his mother insisted on marriage, he wouldn't accept. He didn't like the girls there. He'd say they weren't wife material. Even when they suggested sending him a wife from Iran, he didn't agree. He believed that Iranian girls married for money, status, and ultimately to obtain residency with a man who had it. They weren't willing to leave their homeland for the sake of living together with a spouse.

He wasn't wrong. Girls these days were all rational lovers. Their calculations were precise, and every step was taken with a specific intention in mind. Their eyes were only on their own interests. They behaved the same way in Iran, let alone in Canada, with all its glitters, deceptions, and these superficial girls whose absolute social freedom took away their common sense and made them lose themselves. Living abroad wasn't all for the better. It had its own hardships that might not have existed in this country.

Alas, the inner ape! It knows no rest. It stirs up the whole jungle with its mischief and antics, rattle the vines, and watch what happens. Sometimes it plays, sometimes it laughs, and sometimes it throws you into confusion. If this inner ape allows, Amir would sit down one day and do all the planning. To see which is ultimately better, to leave or to stay? That was the question.

10

Zahra didn't go to the hospital that day. She cleaned and tidied the house in the morning and prepared lunch. Her boss had said there wasn't any need for her to go to the hospital since his mother was being discharged.

Zahra was worried. The old lady was already ill-tempered, and now this whole surgery business made it even worse. Whenever Zahra thought about their argument that day and the old lady's fall in the bathroom, she'd burst into tears. During the days she'd been with her at the hospital in the mornings, she hadn't been able to ask her how she was doing.

It was sure harder to take care of the old lady after that. Perhaps it would've been better to take her to a doctor, so they could increase her medication. Zahra thought that if she couldn't put up with the old lady's behavior, she'd ask Mr. Hekmat to find her another job. Or, even in the worst case, she could leave the company.

She still hadn't been able to find that green scarf. After preparing the lunch ingredients, she searched through the old lady's belongings again but couldn't find it. She'd have to search other areas of the house when she had time and patience. The fridge was empty. She needed to buy a few kilos of fruits, wash, and refrigerate them, along with a box of sweets. There would be guests to attend to.

Poor Mr. Hekmat was a good man, Zahra thought, but the job was eating at him. He told everyone he was tired of it and wanted to shut down the company. Zahra hoped he wouldn't do that, otherwise, everyone would be unemployed.

Zahra didn't get along well with some customers too. During the hours she was at their houses, they expected her not to sit idle for a moment. They couldn't bear to see her take a break. They complained that she was lazy. Whatever something went missing, they blamed the workers. Their logic was that since they're poor and in need of money, they'd resort to must theft.

She felt mortified when they treated her like that. It's true that she was poor, but she had dignity. If she didn't want to maintain it, she had a hundred easier options. Like the women in the streets who made good money with minimum effort. The street women were the lowest class and had the lowest income out of many. The upper ones must make a lot more. There were other jobs too, smuggling, drug dealing, and so on. But she and the rest of the workers kept their honor.

Not everyone was a saint though. Some were tempted sometimes, but they were all human and had the right to be seen and treated as such by others. It's not right to generalize customers either. Iranians have always been religious and from a rich culture. They understood the importance of helping each other and treated others with respect. But no one is perfect. There are also those who've lost their way.

Ever since Zahra met the old lady, she prayed for her forgiveness and health every day. When she realized how the old lady treated her daughter-in-law and sons, her opinion of this family changed a bit. Wealth and comfort can make people lose sight of the right way. People need to be very aware of their selves to avoid that.

They'd called for noon prayers when Amir and Shahram brought their mother home in a wheelchair. The poor old lady couldn't walk yet. She had a history of using wheelchairs, walkers, and canes, since the stroke.

They made a double ramp to bring her up the porch steps and into the hall. Fortunately, the old house was solidly built and didn't have a separate porch like modern duplex houses.

Those were an obstacle for seniors, and patients. Their house didn't have a European toilet at first, but because of their mother's condition, they had to renovate and install one.

When someone's treated in the hospital, everyone breathes a sigh of relief, hoping that the patient's recovered. They don't realize that the effects of the illness on the patient's life begin right after it. The need to be under medical supervision, and may not be able to perform their previous duties at home or work. Even pregnant women might lose their jobs when they go on maternity leave.

No one employs a pregnant woman. They assume that during pregnancy, she can't work like a single girl. Or she goes on maternity leave and expects to receive pay. After giving birth, she'll be busy breastfeeding a newborn, so she won't be able to focus on her work. And then, when the first child grows up, the second one comes along—

It's one of the reasons why girls marry late these days. The bitter reality is that single girls with the highest level of education have a better chance of getting hired compared to married or pregnant women, and mothers. It's harder for women to balance their careers and studies with housekeeping and motherhood. The result, in addition to the rising age of marriage, there's an increase in divorce rates and a decrease in birth rates, which leads to a decline in population growth. In the long term, this will have severe consequences for the entire country, with a decline in young and working-age population.

Zahra was concerned about her own girls. If she could provide them with more support, they'd be able to form a family with less fear and greater enthusiasm. Their passion for motherhood would be more fulfilled. She sighed and continued her work.

This invisible ape within seems to be more than just a jungle dweller. It climbs and crawls on its own. It's unclear how it treats other animals in the inner jungle. It's mostly at the top of a tree. It can't see animals under its feet; rabbits and mice. But a lion's roar can't go unnoticed. It's the king of the jungle after all. Pigeons, sparrows, and falcons are also likely to be noticed, but the underground creatures are a different story. Just like a worm within the earth, no one sees or pays attention to it. Within the ground, it consumes whatever it wants and goes wherever it pleases.

Zahra found several worms in the old lady's flowerpots. The plants had become withered and lifeless since the old lady's hospitalization. Shahram hadn't paid attention to them either. Zahra, however, was aware of their presence. She collected their dry leaves and poured them into the flowerpots. She watered them every week. If there were no worms in the soil, they'd grow healthy and happy with proper fertilizer and irrigation, giving the house a fresher feeling. They'd grow better with attention. Even harmonic music affects their sensitive essence. Like all living creatures, like humans themselves.

Not every living being is always well and healthy; disease and weakness can affect anyone, make them need more attention. In fact, every living creature needs attention and care to grow normally, especially if you want them to thrive and reproduce. Even these flowerpots would wither if not tended to for a week.

Pots should be replaced with new ones, with a balanced mix of fertilizer, manure, and soil. The cuttings should be readied, and at the right time, the soil should be poured into the pots, and the cuttings planted. After a period of waiting, growth would commence and bear fruit. When even a simple flowerpot required so much care, it's clear that humans, the noblest of creatures, with all their complexities, undoubtedly needed much more attention and care to flourish and reach their goals. Only then can one comprehend their immense potential.

Elderly people, like this sick old lady, require more taking care of than ever before, even for their personal tasks. They may even need the help of more than one person. This old woman was proud and stubborn. There's no way she'd play along. She must've been like this her entire life. Sometimes, it was more noticeable, and she was more aware of it herself, but other times, it was less evident and went unnoticed. Her tantrum episodes put her at risk more than anyone else.

11

The company was closed by a court order. It stated that "Amir's Company" was not allowed to operate until the case was resolved. The compliant was a lawyer himself. He tried to reason with the worker, suggesting that she return the stolen jewelry to avoid legal action and court involvement, but the worker denied everything, "Let them investigate me, I'm innocent," she claimed.

The worker had come to Amir in tears saying that the lost item was an old family heirloom necklace with great sentimental value. Amir was conflicted; a treasure could tempt anyone, but on the other hand, the worker's heartfelt pleas made him feel that she was innocent. She wasn't a bad person. There had never been any issues with her before. Occasionally, she might show up late or slack off, but theft seemed unlikely.

Nevertheless, Amir trusted the worker. The company's reputation was at stake. The owner however, wasn't willing to surrender. Being a lawyer made matters worse for Amir. Initially, the client filed a complaint, but Amir and his employees didn't yield. The client had no evidence, and the worker was bailed out. Amir didn't know how and under what law the company was suspended.

The compliant knew that no company would voluntarily damage its credibility and position by backing a thief, but his goal was to pressure Amir to force his worker to return the jewelry. But what could be returned if the theft didn't occur? Perhaps they misplaced it somewhere and couldn't remember, or it'd fallen off unnoticed. Why would they leave such a valuable item where it could get lost and cause such problems? There is an old saying, “Prevention is better than the cure."

Amir was restless. On one hand, he was fed up with the self-serving lawyer, and on the other, he was frustrated with his workers who were causing him so much trouble. In his heart, he believed that his worker was innocent, but he thought that she should've been more careful and handed over such precious jewelry to its owner to prevent it from getting lost. Now, he didn't know how to prove his and his worker's innocence.

The value of the jewelry was considerable. If he were forced to pay for the alleged loss, how much would he have to unjustly pay? While the company was shut down, operations were halted, and there was zero income. This situation was dire; workers would lose their jobs. He didn't know if he'd be obligated to pay his employees' salaries and insurance as well.

This was yet another misfortune that befell him. He'd been considering quitting this job for some time. If only he'd ended it sooner, he wouldn't have been caught up in this mess. He was preoccupied with his mother and son's hospitalization. That delayed his decision. However, as the old saying goes, "A fish is fresh whenever you catch it from the water."

The sooner he quit and looked for a better job, the sooner he'd find one. He'd already decided to leave the country. It was the best thing to do. He was concerned about his mother's illness. It'd take a long time to complete his tasks, obtain a visa, and migrate. By that time, his mother would be fine. Being sick is unpredictable, and news of it isn't always forthcoming. One shouldn't wait for the wheels of fate to turn.

He needed to take action as soon as possible, but the complaint still loomed over him. He had to make sense of the situation. If he couldn't prove his innocence, what would happen then? The other party had their own lawyer, but so what? A lawyer was just a lawyer, after all. Was this lawyer the only one in town? He could hire one too. The judge would see the truth. They wouldn't just accept any argument.

That was the way to go. He had to hire a lawyer. He couldn't handle it alone. He hadn't dealt with the court, the police station, or any places like that before. Filing a lawsuit required experience, and knowledge, not to mention the effort needed to pursue the case, stand before a judge, and what not. He didn't have the patience to wander the courthouse's corridors. He didn't like the atmosphere there or the people whose acts brought them to those halls. There were countless criminal cases involving theft, crime, murder, and so on, making this case seem minor in comparison.

He needed to find an honest lawyer. Not all of them were competent. Some would only lie and deceive their clients for money. People entangled in legal cases would seek help everywhere. He'd be drawn to promises made to him and believe them. He had to find a lawyer with experience, someone whose previous clients were satisfied with their work.

One of Masoud's friends had a legal issue some time ago. They hired a smart guy who solved it quick, got a lot of praise for it. The case was about shopkeepers from an old mall. The original owner, unable to manage his properties, had rented the area to a friend who took care of his affairs. That friend tricked all the shopkeepers into eviction. The original owner passed away, and his children returned from abroad to claim their inheritance. They said that the shopkeepers eventually stayed in their shops without further issues.

Throughout one's life, they may get involved in legal matters a few times. As time passes, this need grows. This new day and age and its people find ways of exploiting each other. To prevent being charged with a false crime everyone has to be aware of the law. Eventually though, they may need a lawyer for their legal expertise, at least for consultation purposes.

Amir didn't know what to do during his unemployment period. He needed a few days to rest and calm his nerves. The past few days had been hectic and exhausting. He longed for relaxation and peace. A short trip wouldn't be a bad idea, but the kids were in school, and he couldn't go anywhere alone.

He had a long list of tasks he'd planned to do but never found the opportunity. He desperately wanted to study, but his mind was preoccupied.

Ever since starting a family and getting entangled in the company, he hadn't found time to read his favorite books. They were on metaphysics and the supernatural, subjects that fascinated him. Among them were a few famous novels that would be great to read in his spare time.

Throughout life's tumultuous journey, one occasionally needs to pause, look back, and assess their path. Every company or institution requires self-evaluation to advance better. As one matured, they had to reflect more profoundly on their life choices. He felt a strong urge for introspection.

Years had passed since he had the luxury of solitude and contemplation. He sensed an inner void, a yearning for solitude and depth. Usually, it was during such times that one found a clearer vision for their life's journey, enabling them to choose their path wisely and confidently move forward.

Perhaps the sense of chaos and discomfort he felt stemmed from neglecting his own needs while shouldering family responsibilities—a wife and two children—realizing how inadequate his efforts had been for his family. He was approaching forty, possibly amid a midlife crisis.

He believed it was important to guide his children in finding their paths as much as providing for their physical and emotional well-being. He wanted them to be mentally and spiritually prepared for life's inevitable challenges.

If they chose to migrate from Iran, adjusting to new cultures, social conditions, and economies would pose a big challenge. Although younger children adapted more easily, the change wasn't always seamless.

Children's heightened sensitivity to their initial living environment made drastic changes more difficult to cope with. One friend faced this exact issue. His Swedish family struggled to adjust. His wife and child moved with him, but their young daughter couldn't adapt, constantly reminiscing about her grandmother's house and the local park.

He, too, couldn't secure suitable employment. After several months, they were compelled to return. Thinking about the chores that had to be done, typically considered men's work—replacing two corroded faucets, repairing the chimney, organizing the basement, and rearranging the orchard. Furniture replacement had been on his to-do list for a long time, but he'd been too occupied. If they planned to leave Iran, these tasks would be irrelevant. There was too much maintenance and renovation work to be done at home anyway. Amidst all the other tasks he wanted to complete for himself, this debacle might've given him an opportunity to make changes in his life.

12

Amir loved preparing chickens. Whenever friends gathered in the garden house, he'd serve them. The cut chicken pieces were sitting in lemon juice since noon, ready for grilling by nightfall. The side vegetables would be grilled beside them. His friend Sohrab gave him a hand with preparing them. Akbar arrived when they were just done.

Behrouz was on his mobile phone all the time. He did most of his trading like that. He carried it everywhere.

Their evening gatherings were usually the four of them. Occasionally, another friend joined, but typically it was just these few.

They'd gather once or twice a month to change their mood. Shahram and his friends came more often. If those guys showed up while Amir was there, they'd sit in the back room. The two groups didn't interact much. Shahram was single and carefree, while Amir and his friends had families and were more responsible.

Shahram's friends insisted on enjoying life while they were unmarried. They said that once committed, their freedom would be taken away. Good thing the garden house was in the city. Occasionally, Amir and his friends brought their families, but for late-night gatherings where wives and children couldn't stay, only the men would come. It let them socialize without worrying about disturbing their families. The garden was their preferred spot.

That night, Haleh couldn't join. She was helping her kids prepare for their exams. The other wives were also busy. The men often stayed up until morning, chatting, snacking, and playing games. It was still dark. They usually had green Ash9 or Kaleh Pacheh10 before dawn. They ate and went home to sleep comfortably in the morning. This happened every Thursday night, as Friday is a holiday in Iran.

Shahram and his friends arrived and went to the lower garden room. They brought fast food, usually pizza from outside for dinner. They didn't feel like preparing kebabs or Kaleh Pacheh.. They were accustomed to a more relaxed and carefree lifestyle

---

9 Iranian vegetable soup with different ingredient like beans and noodles.
10 Traditional Iranian food that consists of a sheep's head and trotters, and is typically seasoned with lemon and cinnamon.

even though their age gap with Amir's friends was small, around five or six years.

They had no major responsibilities, taking things as they came. Their mothers urged them to marry soon, wanting them to settle down. Their laid-back approach was "Whatever happens, happens. Relax!"

People say, "The sooner a boy gets married, the sooner he builds a life." Shahram's mother tried to pressure him, but he resisted. Masoud and Amir tried to convince him too, but he wouldn't budge. He was thirty five already.

Nobody knew what these young people were after, maybe even *they* didn't know. Perhaps they searched for something lost or never found. They seemed more asleep than awake. Maybe they weren't even looking. Or they didn't need to search, perhaps it was with them, but their eyes weren't open to see. Maybe they needed to grow up. Amir was five years older and couldn't find his way, let alone Shahram.

If they had the same problems, they could've helped each other with the solution. Others might have the same problem, even their older brother Masoud. It could be that everyone on Earth has this issue without realizing it. Everyone has a lost thing they need to find. Are people on Earth stuck searching? Can't they help each other or share solutions?

Maybe people don't know they should search. If everyone knew they had something lost they needed to find, it would be a different story. They might not want an answer. Can everyone in the world search for something and never find it? The answer is here on Earth. It's around us. God has answered every question. He's merciful and wise, thinking of everything. Maybe all people need is to want it.

Amir's mind was restless. He sensed an issue but couldn't pinpoint it. He knew something needed to change, but not his family. It was his job. His company closed, and it was out of his hands. He dreamt of a peaceful job, but how? He needed to think, research, and discuss with friends. Gatherings were perfect opportunities for advice.

They brought the chicken inside. Behrouz finished his phone call and started to set the table with Akbar.

Amir placed the tray on the table, "Honorable guests, the chicken awaits your arrival. Come, let's serve them."

Behrouz was reading messages on his mobile, which annoyed Amir. He didn't know where Behrouz got all those texts. He might've been in an affair.

"Can you put away that phone for a second," Amir said.

Behrouz finished replying, switched off the phone, and sat at the table, "Sure thing, my dear friends."

Akbar and Sohrab, exchanged glances and smirked. Sohrab nudged Behrouz, "Hey, buddy, what's going on? Who are you chatting with? Are you secretive with us now?"

"It's nothing but business," Behrouz retorted, "They're just asking me about prices."

"Come on, man, they can get the prices over the phone. No need to read messages."

"Not all of them call. Some prefer messaging, especially when my line is busy."

Amir, wanting to shift the conversation, poured some drinks, "By the way, guys, I wanted to talk to you about something."

Akbar, aware of Amir's work troubles, swallowed a piece of chicken, "You need a lawyer? I know a few. They're good."

"No, I've found a good lawyer. We've talked. That's not the issue now. I want to ask your opinion about my job. I'm tired of this company—the arguments, involvement, and stress. I'm looking for a something better, but I'm not sure what. I wanted your thoughts on this. What do you think?"

"Construction! It's your thing. People rebuild old houses into apartment complexes for themselves and their kids these days. You can do it with a partner." Akbar proposed.

"That's not bad. Masoud is doing it too. I can sell the company assets and make the capital, but he's not stress-free either. You still deal with laborers. I want a job that's peaceful."

"How about real estate? You only deal with owners and tenants," Behrouz suggested.

"It's a saturated market too." Amir replied.

"The food industry— there's always a market. Your stock doesn't depreciate."

|Who has the patience for negotiating milk, yogurt, and biscuits?

"Wholesale, not retail. You supply supermarkets and grocery stores." Akbar explained.

"I don't know a thing about that industry. I don't know where to buy from or sell to."

"You've got an excuse for everything, don't you?" Behrouz said, "You're just tired and don't want to work. Every job has difficulties. You can't quit at the first hurdle and chase after another job. You need to persevere. Your job isn't bad. It's normal to have issues. It'll be resolved, God willing. Take some time off, relax, and you'll feel better."

"That's true, but work conditions abroad are better, for the kids too."

"Ah, so that's the issue. Look, leaving Iran might be a good idea, but timing and destination are crucial. You're at a good age to migrate, but it gets harder the longer you wait. Some places discriminate against Iranians, but others have large Iranian communities. It's easier to settle there," Akbar said.

Amir pondered, "I was thinking about Canada or the US. My cousin is in Canada, so he could be a good guide, but I'm still undecided."

Behrouz encouraged him, "No need to hesitate. Canada is a great choice, better than here—more progressive and industrialized. Once you're there, help us out too."

Akbar smiled, "Alright, Amir. No need to overthink. Take a leap of faith and go. Keep us in your thoughts and prayers."

"Smart ass, you want me to pave the way? Fine, I'll take jump ahead first, then you can follow. It's just an idea now, not a plan. Immigration isn't easy, it takes time."

"Don't waste time, the sooner the better. No need to delay," said Akbar.

"Yeah I agree too," Behrouz said, "For the sake of your kids, you shouldn't hesitate."

"You need to learn English. Hire a private tutor to teach you and your family at home."

"You're right. We'll get a language teacher. What else?"

"You don't have a very useful degree, but you can invest in an independent university for a new one. Find a legal firm that does visa processing. They'll guide you through the process. They'll take care of your visa on your behalf. It should be easy enough."

"I considered immigration through investment, but I don't have the money. I might need to sell my house. It'll take time."

"No pain, no gain. It's worth it, you won't regret it."

"Do I need a lawyer for this?"

"I don't think you do, but I know some lawyers and could ask for recommendations."

"Thanks guys," Amir said before sitting at the table.

13

He was already twenty minutes late. Amir tried calling him multiple times, but the phone was either busy or unreachable. He considered giving up and leaving, perhaps he'd forgotten or maybe he wasn't planning on coming at all. He didn't know the man, only having reached out based on a phone number he saw on a street advertisement. He'd agreed on meeting in the park to have a full conversation.

It seemed a bit suspicious. The lawyer didn't have an office; he said he was in the process of moving to a new location. When

Amir asked about his previous clients, he mentioned having worked in Dubai for a few years. Something felt off, but the guy seemed knowledgeable, citing regulations and mentioning having successfully obtained permanent residence for several clients in the US.

He also claimed to have a visa office with his partners in Dubai, which seemed credible. Amir wished he'd invited him home—it would've been more comfortable and less formal than the park. But, it was his habit not to invite strangers into his house. Then again, this was his lawyer; it was different. He didn't know why the man suggested meeting in the park—perhaps it was close to his new office or home.

It was getting really late, "If he doesn't answer this time, I'll leave and look for another lawyer," Amir thought.

He took out his phone and dialed Mr. Moradi's number once more. This time, he picked up.

"Hello, Mr. Moradi—why aren't you answering your phone? Are you standing me out?"

"Hello, Mr. Hekmat. How are you? Where are you now?"

"I've been waiting here for half an hour, kicking my heels. I was about to leave."

"Leave where? I've put aside all my work to come here just for you. Where are you in the park? I've been wandering around, but I can't find you."

"I can't find you either. Where are you now?"

"I'm at the spot we agreed on. I'm by the pond, but I can't see you. What are you wearing?"

"Black suit and a brown bag—"

"Ah, there you are—"

Upon seeing each other, they hung up their phones and walked towards one another. Amir complained about Moradi's late arrival as they sat down on one of the benches surrounding the pond. Although the weather was cold, they didn't pick a better place for their first meeting. Amir began explaining his work-related problems and why he decided to emigrate from Iran.

"I have a home cleaning and care company for the elderly, disabled, and patients. Everything was fine in the beginning. I could manage it. But every day, there's a new complaint. People lose something in their house and blames it on our employees. Recently, someone lost a necklace, complained, accused us of theft, and got our company shut down."

"How did they do that?"

"I don't know. He's a lawyer too, knows all the tricks. That Goddamn— they put me and my employees out of business.

"Is that so? What's this guy's name?"

"Ferasat, do you know him?"

"No, I don't. If you want, we can offer you consultation—"

"Thank you, but I have an acquaintance who's a lawyer. I spoke with them, and he promised to sort it out. I just came to you to discuss immigration."

"Alright, a company you said. What's it called?"

"Amir Company."

“Oh, I know you guys. My wife hired your workers for house cleaning several times.”

“You did? Sorry for not recognizing you, too many faces, I can't remember all the names.”

“It’s Ok. Did you say you were looking for a permanent residency in Canada?”

“Yes, that's why I came to your immigration office. Please help me.”

"As I explained on the phone, there are various ways to apply for residency, but as I suggested, the best way for you is through investment. It depends on how much money you invest. You can apply for both permanent and temporary residencies. Get your money ready and don't worry about it. I’ll take care of your case in a few months."

"Yeah, that's what I thought too. But the problem is, I’m kind of broke now. The company’s been seized. I have to sell the house. Did you say at least $800,000?"

"Yes."

"I have to sell both my house and a piece of land that I own. That’ll be all I have.”

"Well, when you invest and start working there, you'll be financially secure after a while. There will be some losses at first, since you’ll be spending your savings.”

"Should I prepare the money in dollars or rials11?"

"It doesn't matter. I'll convert it to dollars for you."

---

[11] Iran’s official currency.

Mr. Moradi took a form out of his bag, "For now, please sign this power of attorney form. Your money should be ready as soon as possible.'"

"Do I need to pay more for my wife and children?"

"No, they're covered under your guardianship. When you receive the residency, they'll also be granted the same status."

"Right, I'm sorry for asking such silly questions. I'm nervous. This is my first time."

"Everyone doing this for the first time gets nervous. Don't worry. Everything will be fine."

Amir smiled and glanced at the power of attorney form.

"Yeah, you're right. So, this is the power of attorney form? Meaning, I'm giving you permission to handle all my affairs?"

"Yes, it is. You can read all the terms thoroughly, then sign. If you have any questions, I'll be at your service."

Amir wasn't in the habit of signing anything without reading it first. He began examining the form. It seemed legitimate. Although he didn't understand the legal stuff well, he didn't think there was anything particularly problematic about it. Everything appeared to be in order. He tried to ask a few questions so that the lawyer wouldn't think he was completely clueless and pull the wool over his eyes. He signed the form and handed it over. Mr. Moradi took the form with a smile and placed it in his briefcase.

"You were in Dubai for a while, ha? Amir asked, "What were you doing there?"

"Yes, I lived there for a few years. We had a law firm with some of my friends. We handled immigration cases."

"Why did you come back? Isn't Dubai a better place to live?"

"It wasn't bad, but my wife and children were here. My wife couldn't come to Dubai because of her illness. It was hard for me to be there alone, and my wife had a hard time here, taking care of the children. I had no choice but to come back."

"I hope she gets better, Inshallah[12]. Wasn't Dubai a better option for treatment?"

"No, it makes no difference," Mr. Moradi said with a sigh, "Her illness has no cure, and there's no place in the world where it can be treated."

"Sorry for prying. May I ask what her illness is? It's not cancer, is it?"

"No, it's not cancer, but it's worse." Mr. Moradi sighed, as if the weight of all the world's sorrows rested on his heart. "Anyway, when will you have your money ready?"

"I need to find a buyer for the house and car. The market is in recess, though. The real estate agents will rip you off if they find out it's an urgent sale. I'll let you know when I find a good deal. Is there anything else I need to prepare?"

"Yes, you all need passports. Do you have them?"

"We got them a few years back for a trip to Turkey, but I think they've expired by now."

"How long ago?"

"I think about six or seven years."

---

[12] If Allah wills it.

"Yes, passports expire after five years. It's not a problem, just renew them."

"Ok."

"I also need the original and copies of your ID cards and citizenship cards."

"They're all ready. Do we need to take language classes as well?"

"Yes. Although it's not necessary for a residency through investment, you should still learn English or French for everyday life there."

"Alright, I'm planning to hire a private tutor to come to our house and teach us all. I'm not interested in learning French, though. I heard it's difficult, like Arabic."

"Well, yes. But someone who knows English can learn French more easily. English will do for now."

"We'll leave French for the kids. They can learn it there when they grow up."

"Yes, the children should learn it. It'll be better for their future. Well, Mr. Hekmat, how long do we need to wait? The longer it takes, the more it'll delay your work."

"I know. I'll prepare everything as quickly as possible. The passports need to be ready as well. I think it'll take about a month."

"Send them to me as soon as they're ready, but the faster they are. The sooner we begin the earlier you'll leave the country."

"Yes, I know. You're absolutely right."

Mr. Moradi stood up and extended his hand towards Amir, "Alright. Then I'll be hearing from you."

Amir, shook his hand warmly, "Inshallah, it'll be done soon."

"Thank you for coming. Sorry for the trouble. Do you need anything else?"

"No, thank you. I'm grateful."

"It's alright. Goodbye, sir."

"Goodbye. Hope to see you again soon."

They parted ways. Mr. Moradi went towards the main gate, and Amir headed to the back exit. He was happy that he was building a bright future for himself and his children, but still all the worries vexed him. When Mr. Moradi mentioned his wife's illness, Amir's mind began to wonder. Anyone could fall ill anywhere, but first world countries had better medical facilities for diagnosis and treatment. He'd heard the cost of treatment back-breaking though.

The cost of treatment in Iran is lower than neighboring countries. Iranian doctors are skilled and more knowledgeable, and the healthcare isn't far behind international standards. All in all it's not too bad. Insurance policies also cover many costs. In government facilities, costs aren't a major concern. Hospital expenses for his mother's surgery were high, but that was a private hospital. After all, as the old saying goes, "You get what you pay for."

What happened to his son Dara kept bothering him. The diagnosis was still unclear. They said it was poisoning, but he doubted it. He was afraid it might be a serious disease the doctors couldn't tell, and that it might resurface somewhere in the future. He had to be aware and always save some money for a rainy day.

He could take Dara with him, but what if something happened to his mother while they were abroad? By the time their immigration process was complete and they were ready to leave, his mother's condition might improve. But how many more years would she be alive? What if something happened to her while he wasn't there? If he couldn't do anything for her, would they not see each other again?

Shahram and Masoud were still there of course, but he was sure they didn't care about their mother as much as he did. He'd taken care of her for many years, and now, was he supposed to just leave her and go away? The guilt would haunt him for the rest of his life. But what else could he do? His mother had lived her life, and he couldn't stay by her side forever. Maybe if he wasn't there, Shahram and Masoud would feel more responsible.

Thinking about Mr. Moradi and his wife made him anxious. When he was describing his wife's condition, Amir noticed deep sorrow in his eyes. He really wanted to know what kind of disease she had. What could be worse than cancer? Cancer eventually took lives after a lot of pain and suffering. Whatever was worse than cancer would also take lives, so what was the difference? Perhaps the pain was more severe.

"Whatever it is, may God give them patience," Amir whispered. Mr. Moradi was his age. His wife shouldn't be much younger either. She'd probably pass away in a few years, leaving their children in his care to raise.

It was difficult. He couldn't even imagine it. There was nothing he could do except pray for them. But it was strange. Mr. Moradi was worried, but he didn't even ask for a prayer. Did he not care what happened to his wife? Then why was he worried? Perhaps he wasn't religious and didn't believe in prayers. Iranians who lived abroad for a long time often lost their faith. He was afraid that he and his children would become like that too. So, if someone's wife was horribly sick, would they not even pray for her?

The ape within didn’t let him rest. He’d become obsessed with immigration.

“I shouldn't think too much about possible problems,” he thought.

These kind of thought won’t let go. Once a decision is made, one should focus only on their goal. Any problems that come up will be dealt with in their own time. As an old saying goes, "In doing good, there is no need for hesitation." He’d made a decision, and had to stand firm until the end.

He needed to have a talk with Haleh too. She was his partner and the mother of his children, her opinion mattered. He needed her support. Generally, women are happy to emigrate from Iran for the glamour. Some resist because of their attachment to their family. A few days before, when he brought up the topic with her, she didn't say much. Maybe she needed time to think, but they had to have a proper discussion about it.

14

Haleh was hesitant. She preferred to stay close to her family, but Amir's tried to convince her with arguments about a better future for their children. He understood her hesitation. The younger a person is, the easier it is to adapt to new living conditions. But at her age, it’s very difficult for an adult to leave behind their family, country, home, and to live in a place where they don't even speak the language.

"One of the essential qualities of humans is their ability to adapt to any circumstances," Amir said. "She can find her way in a new environment. It's possible, but first, she has to honestly confront the reality of what she is giving up and what she'll gain instead."

He spoke to his wife and somewhat persuaded her. Then he put their house up for sale at a few real estate agencies. The money from selling the house wouldn't add up to $800,000, but he could get a temporary residence permit with the less. He could stay there for a few years, work, and then go for a permanent residence after a few years. His friends advised him on this, otherwise, Mr. Moradi hadn't said anything. Perhaps because his own plan was for permanent residence only.

Amir wouldn't want to be left empty-handed. There might be unexpected costs. It wasn't wise to put all eggs in one basket. Once the money was ready, he'd consult with Mr. Moradi to see if he agreed with the conditions.

He hadn't told any of the real estate agencies why he wanted to sell his house. When they realize someone needs money, they try to take advantage and lowball the price. He told them he wanted to buy a piece of land for construction. They think twice about ripping you off if you're involved in construction yourself.

He hadn't discussed anything with his mother and siblings. His mother would definitely be against it. Maybe Masoud and Shahram would agree, maybe not. But it made no difference. His decision was final. It was his own life. He would tell them when his affairs were in order. Eventually, they'd understand. He asked Haleh not to tell anyone until before they leave, but women can never keep quiet about things like that.

They'll tell their family, at the very least. And the close friends and confidants too, they make a pact that no one else should know and that it has to remain a secret between them. Suddenly, you open your eyes and realize half the city knew about the news that was supposed to be a secret. This kind of news spreads faster than regular news.

The real estate agents all said the market was stagnant at the moment, that people didn't have money in their hands. His house wasn't very expensive, otherwise, it might've taken a year or more to sell. Real estate agents know their job well. Sometimes they even join hands with the buyer and lowered the price. Or they themselves are the real buyers sometimes, but sent someone else to sit at the negotiation table. They a thousand ways to lie, deceive, and cheat. Only God knows their true intentions.

Do they even think about the afterlife? What answer will they give then? How does making a living out of that satisfy them? Is it possible not to have a problem with it? These sins will eventually gather one day and wash away their house of cards. God's punishment is often silent.

It took a few days for one of the agencies to contact Amir, saying they found a buyer, but he didn't have cash. He wanted to trade the house, to register the deed in his own name and then get a loan on it to pay for his down payment. This'd take at least a few months for Amir to be able to get his money. And, he wanted to buy the house below its actual value. He wanted to have his cake and eat it too. Amir didn't accept the offer.

This type of sale didn't suit him at all. He needed all the money in cash, but he didn't want to tell the real estate agent the truth, so they wouldn't find his weakness and take advantage of it.

How could he get the money soon? His company was shut down. He kept himself busy at home reading books and making the house look good for sale. If it had any defects, that would reduce its price. First, he did some repairs. Haleh insisted on replacing the furniture before, but when she found out about Amir's decision, she stopped. Now that they were planning to migrate, there was no point in spending money on buying new appliances.

They had to sell them anyway, probably at half their real value. It's painful for a person to let go of everything and move to a new place, like leaving this world for another. In migration, everything turns into money, and a person takes it with them to another country. But in the journey from this world to the next, all you take is your past deeds, the good and the bad that have always been with them everywhere. Whatever a person does, they suffer the consequences eventually.

Amir wished people paid more attention to that. The book he was reading was about spiritual worlds. After death, the soul enters another world. That world has different stages, and each person is placed in one of these levels based on their spiritual growth and refinement. In that world, the soul's growth continues.

Like entering a new phase, existing in this world and combining with matter causes a lot of pain and suffering for humans, and sometimes, for the betterment of a soul, it returns to this world and combines with matter to help with spiritual growth and ascension in the spiritual realms. How great it is to live and have the privilege to experience that. People should be aware of that and make the most of it.

It was thought-provoking. When he pondered that, a strange feeling came over him. It was difficult to detach from things he was accustomed to, let alone to separate from them and travel to another world. A journey he'd never thought before to prepare himself, few people do.

He reckoned the upcoming journey would require months of preparation, then there was the distance and alienation to bear. But what had he done for his afterlife journey? Had he spent much? Had he suffered enough? He was ashamed of himself. For several years, he'd neglected his duties, let alone his afterlife. It wasn't like this before. His father raised them to be devout, fasting, and observant of halal and haram. But through the years, he'd become more materialistic and ignored spirituality. Worldly distractions! These were the things that took his attention away.

"But— It wasn't supposed to be like this. In the end, something had to happen somewhere. Change seemed necessary. His life hadn't gone the way he wanted. It was obvious that something was wrong. It was clear that something wasn't right. Things didn't fit together. There was no harmony.

The ape within wasn't getting much done, just roaming around, looking for fun and games, chasing after food, eating from one tree then the next. But what's the point of it all? Is life just about having fun and playing games? Shouldn't there be a goal, a path, a plan? Is life aimless? They say apes are smart, so maybe there's a point to all this wandering. Maybe there's something good in it, if they make use of it. If they want, they can have a purpose. If they seek a path, it might get them somewhere.

Haleh was already preparing herself for the relocation. At first, she was doubtful, thinking about the hardships, but ever since Amir put the house up for sale and some buyers came to see it, she began to accept it. She chose the best clothes they had for herself, the kids, and Amir, and put them in a suitcase.

She wanted them to look their best, not to appear they were from a third world country. She didn't want them to be treated like Afghans were treated in Iran. They could still be recognizable from their skin and hair color. People who didn't know much about Iran and the Middle East thought Iranians were Arabs. She couldn't change everyone's mentality. No matter what they did, these presumptions would still exist. She had to prepare herself to deal with them.

But preparing the kids was a challenge of its own. On the bright side, their minds were clearer and more adaptable to new conditions, but leaving the environment they were used to and accepting the new one was still going to be hard on them.

Amir was worried about Dara's condition.

"Maybe there was nothing seriously wrong," he thought, but how could there be nothing wrong when the child was completely unconscious? If that doctor couldn't diagnose, maybe another doctor could. It wouldn't be bad to have Dara examined and cared for by other doctors."

Delara was a concern too. She was younger and more delicate than her brother. Even changes in the weather could affect all of them, but Delara was more vulnerable, but the human body can adapt itself, so there's no need to worry. From a psychological point of view, it was going to be difficult at first for the kids, but if they were distracted for a few months, they'd get used to it.

There was also the issue of language. True that English or French weren't necessary for a residency through investment, but they needed to learn to live comfortably. Amir and Haleh had taken English in high school and university, but even with that education, they couldn't speak properly at the time, let alone after so many years.

They decided to start from the beginning to refresh their memories. Delara hadn't been sent to language classes yet, but Dara went to language school for a few semesters, couldn't speak fluently though. Amir was thinking about hiring a private tutor, but their levels were different. How would a tutor teach a class of four students with different levels.

For Delara, they had to start from scratch. With no knowledge of the language, she'd have trouble going to school in Canada. She couldn't attend class with kids her own age there, maybe fall behind. Was it worth it? Kids who study in Iran have good theoretical knowledge. But for further education, they have to spend a period in countries with more advanced science.

Even if Delara fell a year or two behind now, it wouldn't waste her time during university. Getting admission to colleges would be much easier for her. Ultimately it was worth it to spend a few years in the beginning and then have a comfortable life. The only worry was the psychological damage she might suffer if she had to attend class with younger kids. Raising a child and sending them to school sure is an ordeal. Rome wasn't built in a day after all.

Parents have to consider a lot, raising their children, for the child to grow up without weakness, disability, or internal conflict, and become the person they have in mind. From the prenatal period, before the child is even born, the struggle begins. It's better if the child grows up to be able to stand on their own two feet when they reach adulthood though, and not need support for the rest of their lives. This is an ideal, but how many children actually grow up to be independent and carry their own weight for the rest of their lives?

15

Amir was overjoyed. The buyer offered less than the actual price, but he was paying cash. He really needed that money. It was the whole reason why he was selling the house. The passports were going to be ready in a few days too. Since everything was almost set to leave for Canada, he threw a party in their garden home, inviting friends and their families. They decided to get together again a week later. He wanted to get the most fun out of his last days in the homeland.

He was supposed to meet the buyer around noon, to sign a letter of intent. It was a pretty lively all-nighter with friends, so he didn't get any sleep, not even for a couple of hours in the morning. He was too keyed up. Eating too much celebration kebab, gave him an untimely ache in the stomach. That Kaleh Pacheh breakfast with the boys made it even worse. There was still plenty of time to digest the food with a walk, before the buyer and the real estate agent arrive. He changed and headed to the park.

The sky was clear, too fair for a winter day. Deep breaths while jogging would help him feel better, burn a lot of calories too. A couple of hundred meters of that and he was short of breath. Not exercising for a long time does that to you. *Or it's just age*, he thought. He paused for some air and began speed walking.

The harder he breathed and further he went, the pain intensified. It was an old ailment, always came much worse after a long night of partying, although never so bad as to need a doctor or any medication. On the bright side, this was a good heads up for him to start taking better care of himself. Now that he had a long journey ahead, visiting a doctor didn't seem like a bad idea. He wouldn't want to fall ill in a foreign country.

The paint wouldn't relent. With every step, it burned sharper, making him unable to walk. Body going frail, he felt nauseous. This time it was different. He had to turn back and hobble slowly toward home. He wished he'd brought his cellphone so he could call Haleh. The soreness and the nausea amplified as he went on, and saliva gathered in his mouth. Finally, he got himself to the curb channel and threw it all up, the taste and smell were awful.

That's better. It was all because of indigestion. Feeling lighter, he continued along the way, caressing his belly. His stomach was relieved, but the intestines were still bloated and in pain. Going for another walk didn't seem so appealing anymore, so he kept heading back home.

He arrived home, glanced at his watch. It wasn't still time for the buyer and the notary to get there. He took the key out of his pocket and opened the door, slumped onto the couch, feeling thirsty. Haleh was busy preparing lunch in the kitchen. He called her and asked for a glass of water. She brought him one, "My God what happened? Did you get robbed or something?" she said seeing Amir's pale, haggard face. Amir explained that his stomach acted up and he vomited once in the street. She insisted that he goes to the emergency room, but Amir refused because of his appointment with the buyer.

Haleh wasn't wrong. Maybe the pain wasn't from his stomach. If it was, he would've felt better after vomiting, but it wasn't getting any better. Maybe it was different than the usual pains after his long nights. She worried it was something dangerous. What if it was appendicitis? Heartburn, vomiting, and all that? If it is, it needs to be operated on immediately, otherwise, it'll burst and—If their appointment was postponed for a few days, nothing would happen.

Finally, Haleh's insisting convinced him. He told the buyer he wasn't feeling well and needed to go to the hospital. It was Friday, and because of the holiday, he had to go to the emergency room. He hoped there would be no serious problem. Amir couldn't drive, so Haleh sat behind the wheel and drove the car out of the garage.

She fastened her seatbelt and buckled the children in the backseat. She didn't dare leave them home alone. She couldn't bear the thought of them being hospitalized again. The hospital environment was an uncomfortable and scary atmosphere of sickness, but there was no choice. It wasn't a bad idea to go to the same hospital where Dara was admitted. Their home wasn't far from it.

When they arrived, Haleh asked the guard to allow her to drive to the emergency entrance. She parked in the hospital garage, helped her husband get out of the car and sit on a chair, took his insurance booklet out of his pocket, then asked the children to stay put and locked the car. She was worried it might take long.

As they approached the emergency room, Amir was sitting on a chair, hunched over, holding his stomach. Haleh took his hand and helped him stand up. They asked for directions, a nurse showed them the doctor's examination room and asked them to go there after giving them a patient number for examination.

Haleh helped Amir sit on a chair in front of the examination room and went to get the patient number. When she returned, the doctor's office door was open. There was no one in line except Amir. He struggled to get up from his seat. Haleh took his hand, knocked on the door a few times, greeted him, and then Amir lay down on the long examination bed.

Haleh looked at her husband, he couldn't even speak. She explained his condition, including the heartburn and vomiting episode. The doctor picked a monitor and started asking questions while measuring Amir's blood pressure. He asked about Amir's age, the stomach pain, when it started, where exactly it hurt, and whether it was constant or intermittent, the doctor put down the monitor and went back to his desk. He asked about any history of illness, previous surgeries, medication use, and family medical history. Amir, overwhelmed by the pain, answered the doctor's questions with Haleh's help. When it was done, then took the insurance booklet from Haleh and started prescribing. It was series of tests. He asked them to bring back the results later.

The whole point of coming to the hospital was to get some painkillers. They insisted that Amir's pain was unbearable and he couldn't tolerate it, so they asked the doctor to prescribe some. The doctor noticed Amir's pale, lethargic appearance and took the booklet from Haleh again. He wrote his instructions on one of the pages and asked Haleh to return to the emergency room after getting the medications.

It looked like they were going to be stuck at the hospital for at least three to four hours. Haleh couldn't bring the kids inside the hospital. She took out her phone from her bag and called her sister to come to and pick them up. She held Amir's arm and took him to the laboratory. They knocked on the door and greeted the staff.

A young lady came forward, took the booklet, and reviewed the tests. She guided Amir to a chair with armrests and entered the patient's name, details, and tests into the computer in front of her. She wrote a code on a small piece of paper and handed it to Haleh for payment. She went to the cashier and paid after entering the code into the computer. The laboratory technician, preparing the blood collection equipment on the table next to Amir's hand, took the booklet and placed on his desk.

After taking the blood sample, the technician poured the blood into two test tubes labeled Amir Hekmat. One tube was placed on a spinning machine with two other tubes. They were given a plastic cup for a urine sample, also labeled with Amir's name. Haleh and Amir thanked the staff and left the laboratory and headed to the bathrooms.

Amir went inside for a few minutes and returned with the urine sample. They handed it over to the lab and headed to the pharmacy. Amir had difficulty standing, he sat on the salon chairs. Haleh went to the pharmacy. While she waited to receive the medication, Amir looked around in wonder.

He was concerned. It was Friday noon, and the hospital wasn't very crowded. The place wasn't bad, they respected the patients and processed their work quickly. The old lady was admitted here for surgery, Dara too. Although Amir couldn't accept the doctors' diagnosis for his son, he was generally satisfied with the hospital. What problem could he possibly have that the doctor ordered both blood and urine tests? They forgot to ask when the test results would be ready. Haleh could follow up on the results in another half hour. It was urgent, so they would certainly be ready sooner.

Haleh returned to Amir with a packet of medication and serum. They went back to the emergency room. It was a large hall with several white-sheeted beds. Most of the beds were empty. At the nursing station, two nurses were busy writing. Haleh placed the serum and medication on the table.

The nurse glanced at the card, asked them to have the patient lie on one of the beds. Amir did. The nurse hung the serum from the chain connected to the ceiling and pressurized it. She inserted the IV into a vein in, and fixed it with tape. She adjusted the serum flow rate, gathered her things, and went back to her desk. Tired of running around, Haleh sat on a bed next to her husband. The nurse wrote a number on a small piece of paper and called Haleh to go to the cashier for payment again.

Haleh took the paper with an unsatisfied smirk. Whenever they came to this hospital, it was the same story with these payments, she was given a code and directed to the—the pharmacy, doctor's office, and laboratory. By the time she returned from the cashier, the nurse had already injected the medication into Amir's IV and left. Haleh handed over the receipt to the nurse and sat on the chair next to Amir's bed.

She remembered her children, and her sister Homa who hadn't shown up yet. She took out her phone to call her, there was a missed call from Homa. She called her back. Homa said she was at the hospital, looking for them. She asked Haleh to wait at the information desk. They finally found each other.

Homa went to check on Amir. She stayed for a few minutes and decided to leave. Haleh insisted that she stay but she said goodbye and took Dara and Delara home with her. She asked Haleh to ask for help without hesitation if she needed any.

Haleh was worried that Amir's treatment would take long, and that they might have to stay at the hospital overnight. The children were going to miss school too, they didn't have their bags with them. When Homa left with the children, she locked the car and went back to her husband.

As soon as Amir saw her, he asked about the test results. She didn't know when they'd be ready. She asked the emergency nurse.

"Usually, it takes half an hour. You could go check now," she replied.

Haleh went there. The results were ready. She asked the guys at the lab about them. They said she should go back to the doctor, so she did. There was a patient in the doctor's office being examined. Haleh waited for him to leave. Then, handed the results to the doctor. He studied them for a few moments, "Which patient is this for? The one with stomach pain?"

"Yes, he has stomach pain and nausea, and you prescribed an IV drip. He's now in the emergency room receiving the IV.

"I see. Their test results are not bad, but there's something suspicious. Will you please allow me to examine him again to make sure?"

The doctor got up and went to the emergency room with Haleh. He examined Amir again, "How are you feeling?"

"Well, a little better, but not much change."

"I'll check on you again when this IV's finished."

"What did the test results show? Haleh asked, "Is it something to worry about? Could it be appendicitis?"

"It's a bit suspicious. We need to monitor it. I'll order an ultrasound for you to make sure everything is okay. Insha'Allah, it's nothing."

He went to the nursing station, found Amir's file, wrote the ultrasound order, and left the emergency room.

16

Haleh's mind was torn between her husband and the children. The night before, she had to stay at the hospital with Amir and only managed to return home once to bring what they needed. She gave Homa the keys and asked her to take the kids so they can pack their school bags. Her sister was a blessing in these circumstances, otherwise, who could've taken care of the children. Homa was always supportive, but Haleh felt her need for her sister even more during emergencies like that.

That night, Haleh had to stay at the hospital again. The night before, Shahram insisted that he stays with his brother, but Haleh couldn't bear staying home alone. She preferred to be by her husband. If she went home alone, worry would consume her. Amir was going to the operating room the next morning, so she decided to stay there for the night.

In the afternoon, after visiting hours, they went to the anesthesia clinic so the doctor could examine Amir before his surgery. The anesthesiologist suggested that it'd be better to reserve a unit of blood, although he mentioned that the surgery wasn't expected to involve significant blood loss. It was just a precaution. He said Amir could be safely anesthetized, and Insha'Allah, his surgery would go smoothly.

Amir's surgery was to be a laparoscopic procedure. They'd make a small incision in the navel. After inserting the instruments through the incision, the surgeon operates inside the abdomen. They were satisfied that the gallbladder would be removed using a modern technique. It'd leave a tiny scar and have less post-operative pain. The surgeon explained all of this to them.

The ultrasound had detected a few gallstones. The doctor mentioned that gallstone pain worsens with fatty foods. Amir's recent episodes of chest pain happened after eating kebab. The surgeon was highly competent and had a kind demeanor; they appreciated his approach. He patiently explained that the gallstones had likely escaped from the gallbladder and got stuck near the pancreatic duct, close to the pancreatic duct opening, causing inflammation.

It was great when doctors discussed everything with their patients, clearly explaining what happened, the recommended treatment, and what to expect. This helped patients feel more relaxed, enhancing cooperation during the treatment process. This way, patients didn't have to repeatedly consult different doctors and face conflicting opinions.

They weren't left confused, ultimately influenced by the kindest doctor or the one suggesting that surgery isn't necessary. Avoiding surgery isn't always the best choice. Sometimes, surgical intervention is necessary, and the sooner, the better. Sometimes patients are more inclined to trust doctors who advised against surgery. Perhaps it was out of fear of acknowledging their illness and need for an operation. Maybe they couldn't accept being sick.

Since being hospitalized, Amir hadn't been allowed to eat. Even after the surgery, he'd have to fast for several days during recovery. His pain had lessened, thanks to painkillers. Nurses said he'd be on IVs Instead of food.

The IVs were mostly water. Did they replace food entirely? What about patients who couldn't eat for extended periods, would they stay on IVs for months? The ape's voice resonated within.

People are so concerned with feeding their bodies, but what about nourishing the soul? Do they know the soul needs sustenance too? Few know of how to provide spiritual nourishment. Even fewer acknowledge its significance. Physical hunger is easy to notice—the growling is obvious—the soul remains a mystery. It is curious. The soul is silence, ignored by many. Sadly, that's the state of the world. Those who speak up are often perceived as weak, becoming victims of injustice. The soul suffers injustice, a more foundational form of it.

Eventually, the soul will speak up, demanding its rights. Although it doesn't speak the language of the body, it will manifest itself. When it finally erupts, people won't recognize it as the voice of the soul. This wailing signals a person's internal struggles—a spiritual crisis. They might say they feel lost, unable to think straight, with no way out. Yet, even under these circumstances, many still won't understand the root of the problem.

Some end their lives in a desperate attempt to ease their suffering. Others who can't find a solution sink into despair. Some eventually discover the path and embark on it, but their progress varies based on their understanding. Some proceed slowly, while others race ahead. Those who nourish their souls are few.

A healthy soul gives them wings to soar high, reaching great heights, attaining sublimity. Those who have reached such heights don't often reveal their experiences, perhaps wanting to keep their discoveries exclusive. Yet, do they achieve this alone? Maybe, it's an inward journey, self-guided and self-propelled.

The silent ones might fear repercussions—external or internal. Perhaps they're wary of envy of those who can't reach such heights. Sometimes, fear can be good, but it can also mislead, causing one to stray from the right path. Those reaching the zenith of spiritual elevation are less likely to be seized by negative fear. Theirs is a positive fear, more akin to reverence or awe.

Amir's fears, positive or negative, could've had many aspects: surgery, unconsciousness, the unknown nature of the afterlife. He was unprepared for the journey—no travel essentials, appropriate clothing and what not—whether it was a journey in this world, like his intended migration to Canada, or a journey to the next. This world is not insignificant, but, as the struggles experienced here may serve as a prelude or a test for what lies beyond. Care and attention are required.

Amir never thought about these things before. He hadn't even considered his own mortality. He was more worried about his mother's death. He was too young to die, or was he? People died at younger ages. Death wasn't about age.

It could happen anytime. Of course, the older a person was, the higher the risk, but the risk was never zero. But why weren't people aware of this? Why wasn't Amir aware? Even the doctor said that the surgery wasn't very risky—the highest risk of complications from the safest anesthesia was only one percent—but every anesthesia had its own risks.

It wasn't without risk, meaning he could potentially die or never regain consciousness. The likelihood wasn't high, but it wasn't zero either. A small part of his mind should've been aware of this. But why hadn't he thought of it before? Had he been wrong not to consider it? Had he been short-sighted about his own life?

If so, then anyone could potentially die at any time for countless reasons. Was it time to start thinking about this? People often don't believe in risks they can't see, and don't pay attention to them. Now that he was sick and needed surgery, fear of anesthesia had made him start thinking about it.

He needed to trust God, for He was his only refuge in such circumstances. The remembrance of God always gave him peace. He remembered his father's worship on the prayer mat. His nightly prayers were never forgotten. He’d inherited the wealth from his father, but what about his character and spirituality?

These should have been inherited too, but where were they? He felt ashamed thinking about it. He promised himself that he would try to become what he should be, but he didn't know when that would happen. He always made this promise to himself when he had a problem, but when the problem was solved, he forgot about it.

The ape within was dozing off a bit. It’d take him a long time to fully wake up, and come to his senses. Then he would jump from tree to tree, branch to branch, searching for food—or maybe food for the soul, that’s good for the ape too. Could they share the same food? The ape and the soul were quite different, but maybe they could help each other. Perhaps he could find food for the soul. He was in a better mood for a task like that.

Amir wanted to contemplate and fight his fears until morning. Haleh was sleeping soundly beside her husband, oblivious to the fears he was experiencing. She wasn't going to undergo surgery, only sit at the operating room entrance. She would feel stressful, but more about herself. She feared losing her husband, protector, and supporter of her children. They were more important to her than anyone.

What a world, everyone wants someone for their own benefit. If they have no use anymore, no one will want them. They say that on the Day of Resurrection, everyone will be bewildered and horrified by their own deeds. This world has become the same. Ultimately, everybody's goal is their own survival.

Is it the same in the spiritual world? Do people want others for their own benefits? Or are they selfless in everything they do? Whenever people want to encourage others to do good, they say things like *What goes around, comes around* or give with *one hand and take with the other* or *Cast your bread upon the waters, for you will find it after many days*. So, every good deed that someone does is with the hope that it will somehow benefit them. Again, it's the same story. Everything revolves around the self, around ego.

It's frightening for a person to see things this way and realize that even their closest loved ones want them for their own benefit. If that person has no use for them, they'll have no value. It's horrifying. Even with a thousand friends, you'll still feel alone. Loneliness is always painful, but if this is the case, why is God alone? Isn't the spirit more at peace alone? Can't it find its food and reach its destination more easily? In loneliness, a person spends more time with themselves, gets to know themselves better.

In the darkness and sleeplessness that had been bestowed upon him, Amir experienced emotions that were new to him. He thought about himself and his life. In this darkness, he assessed himself and those around him with a more open mind, something he hadn’t done before. He perceived things differently, drew conclusions, made decisions of an unordinary nature. This hospital bed was truly something special. It changed Amir's spirituality, his way of thinking, and the outcome of his life.

But he wasn’t going to stay on that bed forever. The surgery would be over and afterward, he’d go home, arrange another meeting with the buyer, and proceed to sell the house and the rest of his plans would follow. But would this illness be over just like that? Would there be no aftermath? Amidst the immigration affairs and taking up residence, did this issue really have to come up? Wasn't there a better time?

What strange things God does. Amir was already suffering from enough problems. What a terrible time for him to be sick. He should’ve dedicated all his time and energy to the other issues. But what wisdom did God's actions hold, forcing Amir to be bedridden at this very moment. Amir couldn't comprehend it. Perhaps there was some reason behind it. Could there be wisdom in illness and suffering when a person is at the peak of their problems? It seemed that the more hardships a person faced, the more they were challenged to confront their difficulties, maybe even to become humble.

But did becoming humble really solve everything? So, where was the wisdom in this? Where could the purpose of this situation be seen?

He hadn't undergone surgery yet, but his stomach pain lessened. It seemed that other patients in the ward weren't in a better situation. Occasionally, he heard the cries and moans of patients in other rooms. Sometimes, they'd yell at the poor nurses. Well, being sick meant enduring pain. The nurses were only doing their duty. It was a hospital after all, filled with discomfort. It's not a place one visits willingly.

The night before, a young man moaned until dawn. Amir didn't know what was wrong with him, but the nurses went in and out of his room all night to calm him down. Haleh woke up a few times too. Both were exhausted by morning. That night, however, there was no such noise. No one else moaned. Amir managed to sleep a bit towards dawn. Not all nights were the same for patients. Some nights were calmer. Other nights were busier, with more patients needing more care. Amir hoped that tomorrow night would be a good one too. He was worried that his pain would be like the patient from the previous night, moaning until dawn.

17

She was relieved that the danger had passed and everything turned out well. She passed a box of sweets around the ward, sharing her joy with the patients, their companion, the workers, nurses, doctors, and everyone else there. Amir's illness wasn't very dangerous, but they weren't accustomed to this kind of thing happening. Neither of them was hospitalized or undergone surgery before.

Although they tried to keep a calm demeanor, especially in front of the children, stress had taken a hold of them from the moment they entered the hospital. Its peak was when Amir was taken to the operating room. When the doctor gave permission for Amir's discharge, both of them breathed a sigh of relief. They were grateful to God that they had the sickness treated before their trip to Canada.

Haleh hugged Amir tightly, her face stained with tears. She'd been anxious about letting him go into surgery, but when her worry subsided, she felt proud. She appreciated him more now that she'd caught a glance of life without him.

While Amir was in the operating room, a thousand questions plagued her mind. Haleh asked the nurses what could be done to prevent recurrent pancreatitis. They assured her that since the cyst had been removed surgically, they didn't have to worry about infection that might lead to pancreatitis. The doctor also said that the chance of recurrence was minimal but not zero.

Haleh took a deep breath. She decided to pay more attention to her husband, and her children's health from now on. Before that, the main reason they visited the doctor was for routine checkups, but they needed to be more mindful from now on. If they'd done preventive sonographies every few months, they would've discovered the cyst earlier, and it wouldn't have come to this point.

To prevent heart problems, people recommend taking an aspirin daily after the age of forty or doing a stress test. Their neighbor said that taking Omega-3 regulates blood lipids. Now that diagnostic facilities have become so accessible and convenient, why don't doctors recommend these measures to their patients? Do people have to experience pain before seeking medical attention?

Isn't prevention supposed to be better than cure? Isn't that what doctors say? But they just sit in their clinics waiting for people to come so they can make money. Why would they prevent patients from getting sick, right? Their livelihood depends it. They won't give up their own bread and butter. So, what happens to the oath they took? Is it all a sham? It is just acting meant to fool honest people?

It was Amir's own fault too. He hadn't thought about having a preventive sonography until he got really sick. How would people know about things like that? They don't have medical knowledge. There are so many different diseases and most are treatable. If all these illnesses could be prevented, it would be great. A full checkup of the entire body, in whatever method doctors deem appropriate, along with a full blood, urine, and excrement test, could help diagnose diseases much earlier, before they become lethal.

It would be time-consuming if everyone wanted to take all these tests every year. Medical centers and pharmacies are already packed with people. The costs would also be over the roof. Maybe these were rumors or just marketing tactics to attract more customers. Even Amir and Haleh's parents were never advised to do these things by any doctor before.

Not everyone can afford the expenses. Poor people sometimes struggle to pay for necessary treatments. It doesn't seem reasonable to pay for such a large number of preventive diagnostic procedures. Maybe they aren't as effective as they appear. In any case, when a disease occurs, it manifests itself through symptoms. Perhaps these are the reasons why doctors don't usually send people for extensive and costly tests.

Humans are often unappreciative and neglectful of the blessings they have and the potentials within their reach. This leads to regret, but unfortunately, this regret arises when opportunities are lost. Blessed are those who realize what God has bestowed upon them early on and appreciate it. But why do only a few appreciate while most don't? Perhaps those few understand because they experience the lack of it, like health deprivation through illness. Those who suffer from disease better appreciate their health. Therefore, illness can be a blessing in disguise for the person experiencing it.

Amir was contemplating things he hadn’t considered before. What if he couldn’t go to work in Canada because of his condition? His capital would be lost, getting permanent residency would be a problem, and Haleh and the kids would face so many challenges. Even if he dies in Iran, they still have properties, that could help Haleh and the kids get by. But what about over there? If he sold the house and couldn't establish his life as planned, he’d lose a lot.

Despite the doctor's assurances about a successful surgery and the unlikelihood of a recurrence, Amir was still consumed with fear. The pediatric specialists who examined Dara assured him he'd be fine. Amir's recent experiences—his mother's, and Dara's hospitalizations—had left him anxious. The doctor insisted that Amir could travel with peace of mind once Dara recovers, but Amir doubted the doctor's words.

Hale's mind was struggling with these worries as well. If it happened there, how would she take care of him? Here, she had her sister to help with the kids, but who could support her there? She worried about raising her children in a different culture. When Muslim children grow up in a non-Muslim society, it gets difficult to maintain their religious values.

Even if they grew up in Iran, there would be generational gap with their parents. Differences are natural. They're needed for human progress. But, the culture gap could be bigger when raising children in a vastly different society like Canada. The challenge for Haleh and Amir would be to strike a balance, helping their children adapt to their new home while preserving essential aspects of their Iranian identity and traditions.

Iranians don't like not being on the same page as their kids. Perhaps they'd find it more acceptable if they experienced them firsthand. You can't truly judge going through it. Haleh and Amir weren't sure how they'd feel about it.

A couple of hours after the surgeon issued the discharge order, the nurse handed them a form and directed them to the billing department for yet another payment. Haleh took her bag and went to complete Amir's procedures. Half an hour later, she returned. She went to Amir's room to help him change his clothes. While at it, a nurse came in with an injection, took Amir's arm, and pressed the cotton ball on the spot, telling him to hold it for five minutes. She then threw the syringe and needle in the biohazard bin and asked Amir for his prescription booklet.

She wrote down the summary sheet detailing his diagnosis, surgical procedure, and prescribed medications. She also gave them instructions for post-operative home care, a list of recommended foods, and scheduled their follow-up visit in two weeks. A small card with the appointment date was included.

After the nurse left, Haleh and Amir gathered their belongings and left the room. Amir could walk unassisted but moved slowly. They paused at the nurses' station, thanked the staff and bid them farewell. Haleh asked Amir to wait in front of the entrance while she brought their car from the parking lot. Once Amir was seated inside, they began their journey home.

The night before, Shahram had insisted staying with Amir until the discharge, but Amir convinced him to go home and take care of their mother. The children had missed their father. The experience seemed to impact Dara the most. He felt his self-confidence and identity were connected to her father's presence.

There's truly no place like home. No place can replace the sense of belonging you feel when you're at home. They felt a sense of ownership and control, knowing that everything within it belongs to them, even if it wasn't perfect. Home can be a city, a country, or even one's own ancestral land. It brings a sense of pride and connection to one's roots. People can improve their homes over time, knowing that it will be there for future generations. Any work done for someone else in a foreign land may bring a sense of accomplishment, but ultimately, the reward is only monetary, and the satisfaction, compared to one's own home is unmatched.

Amir felt a strong sense of attachment to their family home, where he'd spent years creating memories in every corner. Just recently, he made some minor repairs to keep it in good condition. It's not the best home in town, but it was a good place for their family to live, filled with familiarity and a sense of ownership.

Their children grew up there. He reminisced about his own childhood, playing with his brother, Masoud and Shahram, his cousins, and the neighborhood kids during the Eid al-Adha celebrations hosted by his father. All the relatives got together and the kids loved it, playing and fun and Kebab and Kaleh Pacheh.

The honesty and warmth they once shared seemed to have faded away. Everyone had become caught up in their own lives, on earning more money, even though they had enough. Greed had driven a wedge between them, but what was it all for? What could be solved with more money? What pain could it truly heal? Even his brother Masoud owned multiple apartments, but to what end? Who was it all for? He couldn't live in more than one home at a time. The relentless pursuit of wealth had overshadowed the values that once held their family together, leaving a sense of emptiness in its wake.

Perhaps owning numerous homes was a means to display a more vibrant identity, one that might compensate for his feelings of inadequacy stemming from not having children. It explained his relentless pursuit of work and wealth. But does a person's identity truly depend on having descendants? Are those who face fertility issues or choose not to marry are without identity? Is human identity defined solely by material possessions? These things can't be taken to the afterlife—only the spiritual significance one builds throughout life endures. A person's identity becomes intertwined with the meaning they create for themselves, transcending the physical realm.

Amir realized he could only take a few bags and suitcases to Canada. Mr. Moradi would handle the transfer and investment of his assets, but his identity and existence were what truly mattered. As an Iranian Muslim, he reflected on the aspects of his culture and the faith he'd carry with him. At times, the thought of his wife and children adapting to Canadian customs and dress code made him melancholic. He felt a deep attachment to the culture, manners, and traditions of his homeland.

Religious ceremonies, vows, and the rituals to honor of Imam Hussein's martyrdom held deep meaning for him. He'd grown up surrounded by them. Could he bear the estrangement from his homeland? These annual events he once participated in would only be seen by his family through television screens, if at all, given the scarcity of Muslim programming in Canada. Although Iranian TV channels could be accessed from abroad, watching from a distance could never compare to experiencing them firsthand. These bitter thoughts saddened him, but he'd already chosen this path after careful consideration and consultation. There was no use dwelling on it; he needed to focus on his goal and overcome any obstacles.

18

When the language teacher left, Amir picked up his book and kept on studying. They'd arranged for the teacher to come to their home twice a week. When Amir was in the hospital, they hadn't held any classes since no one was home. After about a week, they resumed their lessons. Mrs. Dehghan was a good tutor and an old friend of Haleh's. She usually didn't do private classes in people's homes unless she knew them well.

She'd started teaching Delara the alphabet. First, she worked with her, checked her homework and gave her new assignments. While Delara was busy with her tasks, Mrs. Dehghan taught the rest of the family. They began with a review to refresh their memories and prepare for more advanced conversations.

She was quite effective. In a short period, she set them on the right track. She also gave them some films to watch and listen to for practice.

Women tend to be more patient teachers, especially when it comes to children. Children feel more comfortable with them, maybe because of their maternal instinct. Delara paid close attention to her words and diligently completed her assignments. She knew the teacher was her mother's friend, so she felt the same warmth towards her as she did towards her own mother. Boys are similar in this regard. They establish better communication with female teachers. As they grow older though, they need a more authoritative role model, otherwise, they might lose interest. Teaching has its own subtleties after all.

Amir longed to visit his mother, but he still felt unwell. It had been a week since he last saw her. He was more concerned about his mother's well-being than his own. He was a man, strong, and resilient, capable of withstanding being ill, but his mother was old and sickly. Shahram mentioned that she was doing fine and recovering well, and her physiotherapy had progressed enough that she could walk with the help of a cane. Nurses still tended her for two shifts a day. Shahram tried to stay home more and pay closer attention to his mother too.

The company was closed, but he had the nurses' phone numbers to arrange that. He told his mother that he'd gone on a trip to Tehran, that's why he couldn't visit her. His mother loved him more than the others. Amir was more caring to her than Shahram and Masoud. His mother's prayers were always with him, so his life seemed better than his two siblings. It was difficult to his mother in Iran. He wanted to wait a few more days until he felt better, and then he'd visit her.

He hadn't heard from Mr. Moradi in a while. He promised to prepare the money and send him the documents as soon as possible, but that was a month ago. It was strange. The passports arrived that day. Only the money remained. All they had to do for that was to write a promissory note and receive the checks. He thought he should tell Mr. Moradi. He worried that he might've forgotten their work. He certainly didn't care about them.

He picked up his cell phone and searched for the number then called him. The man didn't answer, no matter how many times he called. Maybe he was upset because of their delay. But no, they signed a contract together.

He was their lawyer. He couldn't avoid answering. Amir called again, but there was still no answer. Maybe he was busy. Amir figured he'll call him back so he scheduled an appointment with the buyer for that week. There was no news from him for several days either. It seemed like he wasn't in a hurry to buy. Maybe the market was bad, or he wanted to put off the purchase to buy the house at a lower price. Maybe they thought Amir had gotten cold feet after the operation, he will have problems and won't be able to work. Maybe that poor man is busy somewhere and couldn't answer. Did that mean both Mr. Moradi and the buyer were busy? Mr. Moradi didn't know about Amir's surgery. Something didn't add up.

He could solve the problem with a call to the real estate and ask to schedule another appointment. He called them. He answered after a few rings.

"Hello, Mr. Jamshidi. How are you?"

"Mr. Hekmat, hello, how are you? Is your family well?"

"Very well, thank you. How are you? Are you doing well?"

"Yes, thank God. Have you recovered? Mr. Karimi said that you were hospitalized before you had an appointment. What happened?"

"Well— On Friday morning, what should I say, I had chest pain since Thursday night. I ignored it, but it kept getting worse. They took me to the hospital by noon on Friday. They did a sonography and said I had gallstones. They kept me there for a few days, did surgery, removed the gallstones, and said I wouldn't have any more problems. I was discharged yesterday."

"Are you better now, Inshallah?"

"Yes, thank God. I'm better. The reason for bothering you, Mr. Jamshidi, is that I wanted to ask if you could please make the effort to arrange a new appointment this week, wherever you see fit, we can finalize the matter and write the promissory note. I also tried to call Mr. Karimi, but he didn't answer."

"Well— Mr. Hekmat. Mr. Karimi has withdrawn."

"Why? Does he want to haggle for a lower price?"

"No, it's not that. On Friday, before they come to your house to write the promissory note, one of their acquaintances took them to see another piece of land— he eventually persuaded them to build on it themselves. That land is nearby, in the alley behind your house. They signed the promissory note yesterday. There must be a good reason why it happened, probably fate."

Amir was surprised. He nodded and took a deep breath, "Yes. Well. Of course, it was fate. Whatever God wills, happens. We must be content with it."

"Yes, don't worry. We'll find another buyer. I was waiting for you to be discharged from the hospital, to recover and allow me to send another one to see the house. There are a few potential buyers. They don't have cash on hand, but if it's ok with you, I can send them to see the house."

"So that's why Mr. Karimi didn't answer my call."

"He probably felt embarrassed to tell you himself. He asked me to apologize to you whenever I saw you and explain the situation."

"No, it's no problem. We hadn't signed any contracts or anything. It was just a verbal agreement. It's nothing. Everyone has their own destiny."

"Don't we all— not to worry, your property is a good one. A buyer will show up eventually. Is it alright if I send someone to see the house as soon as today or tomorrow?"

"Mr. Jamshidi, I'm not going to stand on ceremony with you. I only sell to buyers who can pay in cash. I don't have the patience for installments. I've fallen behind on my work. I want to get my money quickly. Delayed payments don't work for me."

"Of course. You know cash buyers are generally scarce these days. If you want to sell quickly, you might consider lowering the price a bit."

"I said I want cash, but I'm not desperate to sell. If I can't find a suitable buyer, I won't sell at all. I work hard for what I have. Money doesn't grow on trees."

“You’re the boss, whatever you say. If I find a good opportunity for you, I’ll let you know. "

"Do your best please. Whatever God wills, will be."

"Alright, I’ll definitely keep you posted."

"Thank you, goodbye."

He put down his phone, feeling defeated. He was so happy, even planning a party for the week. He’d invited everyone to the garden. Mr. Moradi probably didn’t respond because of the delay. It was understandable. What if he couldn't find another buyer soon? What would he do then? Delaying the sale would mean falling behind. The longer he was behind, the harder it would be. Eventually, the house would sell. Even if it took a few months, everything would work out in the end.

It was unclear when and how things would work out. Maybe it would take a long time. Maybe other problems would come up. Maybe he or someone else would get sick again. How long would this continue? This series of hospital visits and being bedridden, where would it lead? Was it fate or was there an unknown reason for the delay? Was this fate good or bad? Who could be next? God forbid. There's an old saying, third time is the charm. It happened three times already. Could it continue? Hopefully not.

Perhaps there was some wisdom behind these episodes. What wisdom could there be in pain and sickness? What lesson was there to be learned? What good could come from it? Being bedridden, angry, uncomfortable, and in pain affected his family and those around him, not to mention losing money. No matter how he looked at it, all he could see was distress.

Why was he looking for a bright side anyway? Greater evils were being averted this way? Maybe these smaller problems were shielding them from those greater misfortunes. Maybe they were receiving God's grace. Or perhaps it was the evil eye. Their family had always been the subject of envy among relatives and neighbors.

Amir, being the most successful of his three brothers, was likely the target of much envy. Word had already spread about his plans to move to Canada. He hadn't even finalized his application before he started celebrating. But they jinxed him. He rushed it. He shouldn't have allowed news to spread so quickly. He should've waited for everything to be settled and his affairs in order before telling others. Once he's no longer in the country, the evil eyes wouldn't be an issue.

Some narrow-minded people attribute problems to sins, oblivious to their own. They say, Only God is flawless, yet do they not face misfortune themselves? When they face difficulties—even the worst—it's because of evil eye and envy, but when others suffer, it's their own sins, self-serving reasoning is what it's called. Don't they considered that each person has their own destiny and relationship with their God—the God they know—under circumstances unique to that individual? No one has the right to express opinions about it. These senseless judgments they pass are the gravest sin they commit. It's as if they believe they've never sinned in their lives, or consider themselves entirely immune.

Amir didn't think like that, but he knew many superstitious people were waiting for the slightest failure to befall him. Amir didn't pay attention to them, but the gossip disrupted his peace. It would really agitate him sometimes. He attempted to justify his actions with his own reasoning. But sometimes he lost control and got cranky. He had the right to. Dara's sickness and his own seemed like a bad omen. The buyer changed his mind. If no other prospects emerged, what would they do? They might be forced to cancel their plans. Amir had doubts from the beginning. He strongly believed in the evil eye, which is acknowledged in Islam, and Muslims are warned against it.

Sometimes, he went too far and engaged in superstitions. For example, he spent a considerable amount of money buying a few talismans from some obscure online shop. It wasn't clear whether the items sold to him were genuine or not. Or he'd spend a lot on some lucky charm advertised on a channel. Once, he decided to take all of this stuff and throw them away without his wife noticing. But when he thought about it, he realized he might spend the same amount or even more to buy them again.

Possessing these things served no real purpose other than providing a sense of support, along with the belief of achieving their desires. Perhaps this psychological comfort led them to imagine that through magic, spells, and such, they could attain what they wanted. Sometimes, Amir felt sorry for himself. He told himself that if believing in such things gave him solace, then he'll be content thinking they'll solve his problems. Maybe imagining what one wants can guide a person towards their goals.

But isn't there something better than amulets and talismans that could bring peace of mind? There must be some means for believing, right? Can't people visualize their desires through self-belief, self-reliance, and their abilities? Humans, the noblest of creatures, are pure energy. What need do they have for amulets and talismans?

If only he could convince Haleh. Her faith in things like that was so deep that Amir sometimes thought of her as an idol worshiper. People think idol worship is as ancient and unsophisticated, not only does modern idolatry exist, it has numerous appealing names and persuasive philosophies. If only these idol worshipers could see the flaws hidden within their beliefs, they might accept that the true essence lies elsewhere.

19

They'd listed their house with four real estate agencies. Every once in a while, one of them would call them and introduce a buyer. But, none of the customers was paying cash. The market was slow and people didn't have much money in hand. Amir wasn't willing to accept checks; he was in a hurry. It'd already taken longer than expected. Mr. Moradi had turned off his phone. Where had he gone? Maybe he didn't want to complete the transaction, or maybe he'd suspended his business in Iran altogether and returned to Dubai. Perhaps something terrible had happened to his wife.

Amir didn't have his address. When they were at the park, Mr. Moradi said it was nearby, without giving a specific address. He also mentioned that his wife had hired workers from their company several times for tasks around their home, but the customers' addresses were kept in the company, which was closed for some time.

Mr. Zareh was following up with the company's case. He'd given them some hope, saying that it might reopen within days. The missing ring still hadn't been found. He was trying to convince the court that the theft couldn't be attributed to the company. Even if someone was at fault, it didn't make sense to shut down the entire company and leave its employees jobless. Amir, of course, wanted to close the company, but his heart wouldn't let him.

The employees needed their jobs; their lives revolved around it. That crafty lawyer Ferasat must've pulled a few tricks to do it in the first place, that arrogant bastard. Why should a group of poor workers pay for the ego of a self-centered lawyer?

Amir couldn't bring himself to close the company because of the employees. He felt that the prayers of these workers and their families supported his life, the successful surgery, and his mother's recovery. He was still suffering from intermittent pain, but it was much better than before. Just as they had explained during his hospital discharge, fatty and heavy foods weren't good for him. He ate fewer eggs and poultry.

His pain would surely diminish over time, but it was persistent for now, flaring up occasionally. His medications had run out a few days ago. It was time for his follow-up visit. When he met with the doctor, he asked for a new prescription.

His medications weren't anything special, just some antibiotics and painkillers. His stitches were still there. His pain was likely because of them. The surgery was successful, so there shouldn't be any other problems. All that was left was a doctor's visit and the removal of the stitches.

Amir felt better and tried to take a walk to the neighborhood park every afternoon, where he'd rest for a short while before returning home. Haleh insisted on going with him to the doctor's appointment. She wanted to be there to hear the doctor's opinion.

Amir went for a run, something he could do again. He observed the streets and shops with a unique interest, thinking he might not have the chance to see them again for the rest of his life. The parks, trees, flowers, historic buildings – everything in this city was full of memories. Every corner of the city held a chapter of the nation's history. It was Shiraz, the city of mysteries.

Where in the world could one find such mysteries? Even if they existed elsewhere, perhaps they wouldn't appeal to someone from a different nation. Each nation's mysteries align with its own taste. Perhaps they're connected to their essence. But how could that be? Aren't all people human? Don't we all share the same parents? If we share the same parents, why do different races have such distinct characteristics?

Their skin color, customs, culture—everything is different. But what about their essence? Is that also different? If people's essence varied that greatly, we couldn't call them all human. Humanity is consistent across cultures and beliefs. It has no particular color or pattern. It demands unity, focusing on serving the Almighty. The core principles and ethics of humanity are universal. They don't differ from one city to another, one country to another, or one race to another. So where do these differences originate from?

They were approaching the doctor's office. It was great that he had an office. Crowded government hospitals were a big pain for patients. There, they'd have to wait for months for their appointment. On the day of their appointment, they'd have to wait all day, from morning until late evening or midnight, for their turn. It was much more comfortable at private offices. Patients could call to schedule appointments, and the doctor could spend more time with his patients. It was probably more comfortable for the doctor as well. Of course, the cost of a private practice visit is higher than a hospital visit, but for busy people with little free time, it was worth the expense.

They parked the car in and entered. The office was on the third floor of a five-story building. The hallways were empty, and the entire building was quiet. Amir was the third patient. They waited for half an hour until the doctor arrived. The doctor likely didn't see many patients and perhaps didn't even reach twenty by the end of the day. How did he cover his office expenses?

It took quarter of an hour for the first two patients to finish their appointments before it was Amir's turn. He stood up with the help of Haleh, and they entered the doctor's office. The doctor stood up to greet them. After exchanging pleasantries, they sat on the chairs. The doctor remembered Amir and the details of his surgery, so there was no need for further explanation from Haleh.

"Yes, I remember. So, how is he doing now? Has his pain subsided?”

Amir thought he should answer the doctor's questions himself, "Thank you, doctor, I'm feeling much better." He placed his right hand on his navel, "But I still feel a bit of pain around here, near the surgery site."

The doctor looked surprised, "The surgery site is painful? Please lie down on the examination table so I can take a look." Amir nodded and went to the table. He pulled up his clothes and lay down on the table. The doctor got up and approached him, putting on a pair of latex gloves.

"Has the pain been constant all this time?"

The doctor examined the surgery site and the surrounding area, "Your stitches look good. Does it hurt more now?"

Amir was trying to carefully compare his current feelings to the constant pain he had before, "No, doctor, it doesn't hurt. It's mostly here. And it goes upwards."

"Do you also experience nausea and bloating?"

"A little, not too much."

"What about vomiting?"

"No, not at all."

"Alright, please come with me."

Amir got off the examination table, and sat on the chair beside the doctor's desk. The doctor wrote on a small piece of paper to have Amir's stitches removed, "Give this to the nurse."

The doctor began writing a sonography request in Amir's file and explained that the pain was likely unrelated to his surgery or previous condition.

Haleh felt anxious , "What could be the issue, doctor?"

The doctor smiled reassuringly, "Don't worry. It's probably nothing serious. I offered it just to make sure everything is okay." He handed Amir's file to him, "Here you go. Please get the sonography done as soon as possible and bring me the results." Amir took the file reluctantly, "Do I need to be on an empty stomach?"

"No, you don't need to be. Two blocks down, there's a radiology clinic. You don't need an appointment. They'll do the sonography for you immediately. Just make sure to bring me the results on time."

Haleh and Amir thanked the doctor and left his office. They headed to the nurse's station, handed the small piece of paper to the nurse, and she guided them to a room labeled Suture Removal Room. Amir lay down on the bed, and the nurse began removing the stitches. Once she finished, Amir got off the bed, fixed his clothes, and thanked the nurse before saying goodbye.

He knew where the radiology clinic was. He and Haleh got in the car and drove to it. Luckily, it wasn't too busy. Haleh handed Amir's file to the receptionist, "The doctor said we need the results as soon as possible."

The receptionist found the sonography request page in Amir's file, "Alright. The doctor is currently performing a sonography. You'll have to wait a little bit."

"That's fine. How long?" Heleh asked.

"About thirty minutes— maybe an hour."

Haleh nodded, "Okay, we'll wait."

The receptionist started entering Amir's name and information into the computer in front of her. Then, asked Amir to pay the fee. Amir handed over the money, the receptionist counted it, then gave them a receipt along with the file, "Please have a seat. I'll call you when it's your turn."

"What could it possibly be?" Haleh asked her husband.

"I don't know. The doctor didn't say anything specific. These doctors play it safe. I don't think it's anything serious."

"They're just being cautious. It doesn't hurt to be cautious. We'll do the sonography to make sure everything is okay. God willing"

Haleh took a prayer book out of her bag and started reading. Amir sat back in his chair, resting his head against the wall. He wondered, "What could've happened that would need a sonography? The gallbladder was removed. Could there be another infected cyst?"

He couldn't figure it out. He didn't know what was inside the abdomen. He studied mathematics in high school, not biology. Those doctors, they pick up a knife, cut open people's abdomens, and put their hands inside. That takes courage.

After about forty-five minutes, they entered the sonography room. The doctor was explaining the results of the previous patient's procedure on a voice recorder. His assistant would type it later. The assistant removed the sheet from the bed and replaced it with a new, clean one for Amir to lie on.

Once the report was recorded, the doctor came to the bedside. He glanced at the files in front of him, "Are you here for an abdominal sonography?"

"Yes, doctor," Amir replied.

"What's your condition?"

Amir gave a bitter smile and explained to the doctor that about two weeks ago, he went to the hospital with pain, and during a laparoscopic surgery, his gallbladder was removed. But he was now experiencing pain in the middle of his abdomen. The doctor applied a colorless gel to Amir's belly where he felt the most pain and began examining it with a probe. After about five minutes, he handed Amir some paper towels to clean up.

Amir anxiously asked if there was any serious problem. The doctor casually gave a brief pause and said he hadn't noticed anything unusual and that his sonography results were normal, then he started recording Amir's sonography report, Amir and Haleh thanked him and left the room. The secretary asked them to wait a few minutes while she prepared their written report.

After a few minutes, the written report was prepared, and the secretary handed it over in a folder.

They finally left the clinic. Amir was pleased that the doctor hadn't found anything wrong. When the surgeon asked him to get a sonography, he was worried sick. But now, he was fine. The doctor was probably still in his office. They returned to the him, luckily, it was still open, and there were only a few patients waiting. They showed the sonography result to the secretary. She asked them to wait for a few minutes.

They didn't have to wait longer than five minutes. Thankfully, both the clinic and the radiology center weren’t busy that day. This is why Amir preferred private clinics. They entered the doctor's office and greeted him.

“They told me it's nothing serious," Amir said.

The surgeon asked them to sit on the chairs and started reading the report.

"Fortunately, there were no issues in your sonography. Your pain is not related to the surgery. It's an internal issue. But you need to see an internist for sure. I'll write you a referral letter for Dr. Parsa. He’s one of the best in their field. He’ll surely be able to diagnose the cause of your pain."

"Excuse me, doctor. What does it mean that it's not a surgical issue but an internal one? What kind of problem could it be?" Amir asked.

"It could be related to your pancreas or stomach. Or maybe it's not a significant issue at all."

"But you said that I wouldn't have pancreas problems after the surgery!"

"I meant acute inflammation, but now I suspect that your pancreas might have a different underlying problem."

"What kind of underlying problems?" Amir asked.

"For instance, your pancreas might not be functioning as it should."

"Why could this happen?"

"There could be various reasons. It could be hereditary, an issue that has developed over the years, or related to a particular lifestyle. There could be numerous factors involved," the doctor elaborated.

After he finished writing the letter, he handed it to Amir, "I've described your condition in this letter. Make sure to consult with doctor Parsa."

"Where is Dr. Parsa's office?"

The doctor took the letter from Amir's hand, and wrote Dr. Parsa's hospital's address on the back, "He doesn't have a private office. He's a full time university professor. I've written the hospital's address for you on the back."

Amir didn't like government hospitals, "Is it possible for you to refer us to a doctor who has a private office? It takes a long time to get an appointment at a government hospital."

The doctor smiled and handed the letter to Amir, "No one is more reliable than Dr. Parsa. It's worth it. You won't regret it."

With a heavy heart, Amir took the letter from the doctor and left.

20

Being unemployed upset him a lot. His heart ached for work. Despite all the hardships, it had its merits. He'd gotten used to it. He didn't notice that before. Now he realized how attached he was to that job. His yearning for the company wasn't only financial. It was more spiritual. Seeing that he could be a helping hand to many people, he felt a sense of satisfaction. It gave him self-esteem.

The pay wasn't bad either, but now he felt a greater need for things other than money. With a little patience, his problems wouldn't be unbearable either. Maybe continuous work had exhausted him. If he took a break, once a month or every two or three months, his resistance to tolerate problems would be greater.

It'd been a long time since he paid attention to his inner self. He hadn't analyzed his desires, and aspirations. He'd been careless. Now that he was scrutinizing, he realized that he had everything, or at least the best things. It just required some patience and attention. Comparing his life with that of his friends and brothers, he wasn't behind, perhaps even ahead. The same was true for his cousin who lived in Canada. You have to let go of some things to make room for others. You can't have everything all at once, this is the universal law.

He'd been ungrateful for years. Throughout his life, he'd never properly acknowledged any of God's blessings, never known their value. He had good health and a loving wife and children, and his life was on track. He'd also forgotten the blessing of serving others. What a blessing it was, the source of a thousand good deeds. Nothing supports the spirit and its sublimity as much as a benevolent prayers from people. He never thought about it before. Why?

Maybe he didn't know how to do it. If something is important to a person, they can find a way to pay attention to it. When there's a will, there's a way. So it was his own fault. He hadn't wanted it himself.

It's emphasized in the scriptures that people should pay attention to their inner thoughts as well as action. All of them ultimately return to the person themselves. Bad thoughts don't yield good results, let alone bad actions. Good thoughts bring blessings, just like good actions. In Islam, even the intention to do good deeds is considered a reward, so that people are mindful of their thoughts, think beautifully, see beautifully, and ultimately live beautifully. Not outward beauty, but inner one. A change of perspective is needed.

What would they do in Canada? Are there blessings there as well? From a material perspective, it could definitely be better there, but what about spiritually? They may not be Muslim, but neither are they disbelievers. They believe in some scriptures, Christians or Jews, who believe in God and the afterlife. So they shouldn't be spiritually inferior. But perhaps they lack richness. Since Islam is the last and most complete religion, and Prophet Muhammad is the last Prophet, perhaps their spirituality is as refined. Not many people here pay attention to spirituality in the way they should either.

There's always been a difference between East and West in terms of focusing on nature and higher powers. Westerners often don't accept these things, or don't pay attention to them. Paying attention to nature, metaphysics, the universe, the mind, and thought is mainly associated with Eastern cultures.

In worldly matters, they're doing well, and they say that a person can become whatever they desire. Whoever desires the world, reaches the world, and whoever desires something else, won't receive anything but that. How much potential do humans possess? If whatever they desire becomes reality, then why don't they desire the best? Why are they satisfied with mediocrity?

The more he thought about it, the more uncertain he became. Now, beside his concerns about spirituality, he was also worried about falling behind on it. He and Haleh had grown up in Iran, and they weren't willing to lose their culture and morals for the glitz and glamour of Canada. But children who grow up there will be more like the people there. He was worried about the future of his children, and whether they would turn out well or not. Would his children end up in an unsuitable educational environment? Would that make him feel ashamed before God for failing to raise them properly?

It was difficult to make a decision about anything. The more important the issue, the harder the decision becomes. It had taken over his life. A great journey, migration from one country to another, from one continent to another, had taken over his life. Every moment, a new thought occurred to him. With every event, he considered another aspect of the story and saw it from a different perspective. He wished he had someone to consult with.

But who? He wished his father was alive, but if he were, he would definitely disagree. There was no need for consultation. He knew his father's opinion. His mother was also definitely against it. His brother Masoud was more likely to disagree than Shahram. It's interesting how the older people get, the more they disagree with migration. Maybe they get used to where they are. The younger they are, the easier it is to leave.

Leaving this world is similar. The less you stay in it and the less attached you become, the easier it is to leave. The heavier the material burdens, the harder it is to leave. The younger you are, the more flexible and adaptable you are. The older you are, the harder you become. How was he? He was nearing forty. He had either reached or was reaching mental maturity. He was neither young and inexperienced, nor old and stubborn. The harder ones break when faced with opposing forces. The younger ones can withstand and bend but don't break. He wasn't old and stubborn yet. He could still resist. He hadn't broken yet. One by one, he found and solved his problems. But first, he had to prioritize. First came health, which was the foundation. If he was healthy, he could solve his other problems. If he lost his health, other problems would follow.

He took the doctor's letter, a referral to Dr. Parsa. He hadn't heard his name before, but his surgeon highly recommended him. He must be good. It wasn't for no reason. Doctors themselves know each other best. He needed to go to the hospital, but he knew it would be a hassle. University affiliated hospitals are too busy to see patients promptly. The doctors were good, but they were always booked for months.

Amir didn't have time to fall behind on his work for months because of the doctor's schedule. The first visit would surely need tests. By the time the test results were ready, the second visit, treatment would start, and it would take months to see results. He didn't have time. He'd already wasted a lot of time.

He wished he could find a specialist with less demand so he could get an appointment sooner. But the better the doctor, the more crowded their office. In Canada, he could find better doctors. Maybe it wouldn't be so much of a hassle. It would take a long time to settle down there and learn the ropes. Maybe this pain would worsen, and he wouldn't be able to leave. Maybe this illness would create problems that would make traveling difficult.

There was no time. The sooner he got to the doctor, the better. Maybe his appointment wouldn't take too long. If they delayed, he'd find the doctor himself and explain his situation. Maybe he'd agree to start his treatment sooner. He was persuasive. Most doctors are influenced by their receptionists. That's how it is in Iran, a janitor could be more persuasive than the boss. He had to see the receptionist first.

He got dressed and headed to the clinic. On the way, he thought about how he could speed up the process. The clinic was on the fifth floor. The elevators were so crowded it couldn't go up. It opened and closed several times, and a few people got off before it finally moved. Those who could, took the stairs.

He preferred to climb the stairs instead of waiting too. He walked with a limp, but he could still climb the stairs. At each floor, he paused for a few seconds, took a deep breath, and continued. Finally, he reached the fifth floor. He was thirsty. There was a water dispenser in the corner of the wall. It was cold outside but the clinic was so crowded, that he was short of breath all the time. He went to the dispenser, took a cup of water and poured some water.

A couple of receptionists were sitting behind the desks with different doctor names above them. He found Dr. Parsa's receptionist. She was a middle-aged irritable woman. Patients were talking to her. He greeted her warmly but was met with a cold response. He gave her the surgeon's letter and requested an appointment, with a lot of flattery. The receptionist glanced indifferently at the letter and closed the notebook in front of her without looking at Amir, "I can't give you an appointment sooner than a month and a half."

“Mam, I’ll be dead by then. I’m planning to leave the country. In a month and a half, I won’t even be in Iran. Please do me a favor and give me an earlier appointment.”

“Everyone says that. There are many patients. You can see there is no earlier appointment. We’re giving patients appointments six months in advance. One and a half months is already good for the first visit.”

“My condition is urgent.”

“Everyone who comes here has an urgent situation.”

“Let me talk to the doctor. I'll get permission from them.”

“It's not possible. Even if the doctor says I can't give an earlier appointment.”

“Oh man. Lady, why are you being so difficult? “

“Sir, do I write your name down for a month and a half from now?

"Fine, but—"

“There's no but. This is all we can do.”

“Alright, thank you. “

She wrote down the appointment date and the doctor's name on a small piece of paper and handed it to him. She told him to go for blood work, get a medical file, and register on the day of the visit.

Amir was not satisfied. His efforts were unsuccessful. A month and a half later was too late. There had to be a way. It would be great if he could find a connection. He thought about it, but he didn't know any doctors personally or have close friends or family at this clinic. He went downstairs when his eyes fell on the charity box. He wished he'd seen it when he came in and dropped some money. He reached into his pocket to see if he had any spare change, pulled out his wallet and checked. He didn't have smaller than five hundred tomans[13]. He took out the bill from the money pile to put in the box. He paused, noticed a few large bills, then went back up. Money solves all problems, but this was a government hospital. It was worth a try.

He folded his surgeon's letter with the money in it and returned to the fifth floor. A few other patients were standing, arguing with the receptionist about their appointment times. He approached again, greeted her, and placed the letter on her desk. She gave him an angry stare, "You're back again!"

"Please read this letter."

She realized what he intended, took the letter and put it in front of her. She opened her notebook, wrote down a visit time for that same day, and handed him the paper, "Here is your appointment, sir."

Amir checked his appointment time. It was for the same day. He hurried to the registration desk. When his turn came, he placed his insurance booklet and appointment slip in front of the clerk,

---

[13] The unofficial currency of everyday transactions in Iran.

paid the fee, took the receipt and returned to the receptionist. The money he'd given to the receptionist was much more than what he paid for the doctor's visit. The receptionist took the receipt from him, "Please sit. I'll call you."

Amir figured he might be the last patient.

"When's my appointment?"

"You're the last one, sir."

"So, I can go home and bring my papers?"

"If you come back quickly."

"Thank you."

They say money can't buy happiness. How could he get an appointment with a bribe then? People change their minds when they see the color of money. Every locked door can be opened by the magic of money.

Amir happily went to the parking lot, got into his car and went home. He found the hospital documents, the discharge summary, and the medical report.

Haleh saw him with the documents, "Did they give you an appointment for today?

"They wouldn't first, but I got it eventually."

"How?"

"Like this!" Amir said rubbing his index finger and thumb together.

Haleh gave a sad sigh, "Do you want me to come with you?"

"No. Stay home with the kids. It'll probably take until the end of the night. Have dinner. Don't wait for me."

"Okay. Don't worry."

"Thank you. Goodbye."

Haleh didn't have the patience to go with him this time. She knew it wasn't anything serious. His sonography didn't show anything serious. The doctor said it. Doctors are in the habit of prolonging things. It'd take until the end of the night and she couldn't leave the kids alone.

Amir returned to the clinic. He went up the stairs to the fifth floor, went to the receptionist and asked if it was his turn.

"You're the last one," she said indifferently and pointed to the chairs in the middle of the hall.

It was crowded. All the chairs were full. The last chair in the hall next to an old lady was empty. The old lady was alone. He said hello and sat next to her.

He started looking around. There were so many patients. He didn't like this crowd. If he didn't have to, he would never come here. There were so many sick people, and the air was thick. People were coughing. It was the flu season. After sitting there for a few minutes, he felt like he was inhaling viruses into his respiratory system.

The announcer in the patients' hall called the names in order. The Amir looked at his receipt. His turn was number sixty. He decided not to stay in that polluted waiting room. He came down the stairs and started walking around in the yard. It was hard to wait. The air outside was colder. He sat on a bench. Patients and their companions were coming and going. It was already night.

They brought a young man on a stretcher. His eyes were open but he seemed limb. His gaze was fixated on the sky, as if waiting for something or someone. Maybe he believed a heavenly misfortune had inflicted him and was watching the sky to make sure another calamity wouldn't strike without his notice. Four men were with him. Their humble appearance made Amir's heart ache. There's a saying; *when it rains, it pours*. Those poor guys were already miserable, now they had to take care of that young man too.

It got colder quick. Amir stood up and started walking, rubbing his hands together. He noticed a father carrying his paralyzed child out of the hospital. The boy looked about ten years old, looked like he had a brain seizure. His mother followed behind, carrying a bag. Sometimes people remain bewildered by the will of God, questioning the wisdom of children being born with congenital problems. What was the purpose of their existence in this world, filled with agony, suffering, and discomfort? What benefit did they bring to their families, apart from misery, pain, anger, and depression? Perhaps that was precisely why they were brought into the world—to test and strengthen of their families and those around them. To elevate one's soul, hardship must be endured. Humans come into this world with pain and suffering, grow and evolve through it, and ultimately reach a higher state. After all, growth and transcendence are impossible without pain.

Amir was tired of pacing. He returned to the clinic. It was slightly less crowded now. He took out his mobile phone to entertain himself with games. He also installed a chess app. Waiting was exhausting. He there was something to do for patients who had to sit there, like an educational film, book, magazine, or newspaper. There was a television in the corner, but it was so noisy. He remembered a newspaper kiosk near the clinic's entrance and went outside again. It was still open, so he bought a newspaper and went back inside. The clinic loudspeaker announced that patient number fifty was to go inside. It was still a while before his turn would come.

He opened the newspaper and began reading. First, he read the main headlines on the front page, then went through the finance, digital, real estate, tourism, and sports sections one by one. He read the headlines and, if he found an article interesting, he'd read the whole piece. He read the entire sports section. He was also interested in arts and cinema, but the economic and stock market analyses captivated him the most. He had a passion for the stock market, but since he couldn't pursue it as much as he would've liked, he hadn't dived into it yet. Shahram hadn't achieved anything to motivate him either. Maybe if he pursued it on his own and learned the ropes, he might've done better.

Most of the lounge chairs were empty now. He looked at his watch; it was midnight. He was anxious about the doctor's diagnosis. He'd never heard of a case where the pancreas malfunctioned, causing chest pain.

The lounge loudspeaker announced number fifty-nine. His mobile phone rang; it was Haleh.

“Hi. How are you? Is everything alright?"

"Yeah. Did you see the doctor?"

"Not yet. It's not my turn yet."

"You haven't been seen yet? When is your turn?"

"It's coming up. You should sleep. Don't worry. I'll be home in half an hour."

"Alright. I put the kids to sleep. I'll wait for you. Take care."

"Okay. Thanks, Goodbye”

"Goodbye."

Haleh was more worrisome after his surgery. When he didn't come home before, she wouldn't call to check on him. But now it was different. Maybe now she appreciated her husband more. The more she paid attention, the more her love on Amir grew. She was a woman, after all. She knew a thousand ways to enter a man's heart.

The loudspeaker announced patient number sixty, making him snap out of his sweet dreaming of Haleh. It was finally his turn. He was the last patient. He picked up the newspaper and documents and went to the doctor's office. Another patient was still inside. He waited for that patient to come out, and then he entered.

Doctor Parsa was a middle-aged man with grayish hair and stubble. His glasses and strands of white hair, gave him an air of experience. An aura of exhaustion lingered on his face; he certainly hadn't found the time to shave. A part of his white coat was caught under the frame of his robe. Doctors sure are too busy to take care of their looks, their health, or their families. People think doctors don't get sick, but in reality, they're probably more prone to disease.

After exchanging greetings, Amir placed his medical file on the doctor's desk. He started explaining his problem - the initial stomach pain, hospitalization, and surgery. He mentioned that the pain continued to bother him. Doctor Parsa read through the surgery report and hospital summary. He then asked questions about Amir's family medical history, and history of prior illnesses. Amir answered all the questions. When asked about the location of the pain, any accompanying symptoms like nausea or vomiting, and if it worsened at certain times of the day, Amir couldn't discern a specific pattern.

The doctor asked Amir to lie down on the bed. After the examination was done, he scribbled some notes in Amir's medical file and handed it over to him. They were some blood and stool tests. He also mentioned the possibility of Amir having pancreatic necrosis and impaired pancreatic function. Amir nodded in agreement since his surgeon had a similar suspicion. He wanted to know the reason behind his condition, but Doctor Parsa postponed further explanation until the test results were ready.

The doctor recommended a reliable lab for the tests and gave him an appointment slip for the following week. Amir was happy he wouldn't have any trouble scheduling. He left the doctor's office.

The streets were completely empty. An unusual tranquility reigned over the city. Amir loved it. He listened to a gentle instrumental track in his car. Driving in the quiet darkness with this soft music relaxed him. He really needed that. He wished he could drive like that until morning. Maybe that's why young people enjoyed driving at this hour, he thought. Some of them acted recklessly. With those loud horns installed in their cars, blaring music, sports exhausts, and tires, they'd get on everyone's nerves. These young people have a world of their own, a world Amir didn't understand. Maybe this was just a phase some young people went through, a phase they needed to feel young.

21

The old lady was more peaceful now. She wasn't as grumpy as before and her mood swings happened less often. Maybe it was the effect of her illness. It made her stronger in the face of life's problems. She appreciated what she had, things she hadn't thought about before. She also recognized her shortcomings as a person. It'd been over a month since her surgery. She could walk with the help of a walker now, just like she could walk with a cane before the accident. The physiotherapist visited her daily for sessions.

Zahra came in the mornings and stayed till the afternoons. Shahram also tried to be home in the evenings more often. He didn't hang out with his friends as much as he used to. Maybe he felt his mother's absence more and wanted to make the most of their time together. After all, he was the youngest and had a deeper emotional connection to their mother compared to his siblings. The old lady also cherished him more.

Amir, however, showed a different kind of respect to his mother. If Shahram was still like a sweet toddler in his mother's eye, Amir was like a mature and reasonable man. He was attentive in every way. He arranged for a nurse, made sure she took her medication, and even brought his siblings together. He wasn't the eldest in age, but he was the most responsible in their family. Masoud didn't bother with these things much. Not that Zhila let him. Whether it was out of jealousy, selfishness, feminine cunning, or a cover-up for her own deficiencies, she didn't like mingling with her husband's family.

Despite his own illness, Amir visited at least twice a week. He talked to his mother and listened to her. The elderly need more attention as they age. They yearn for a child, grandchild, friend, or acquaintance to visit. The old lady found solace in Amir's presence. She expected him to take her worries away, but Haleh brought up the children's classes and lessons as an excuse not to visit.

The old lady's illness had a profound impact on her temperament. This wasn't the first time she got sick. Every misfortune brought changes to her demeanor. First, her husband's death mellowed her arrogance and temper, but not completely. When she suffered a stroke, it all changed a lot. She couldn't accept these hardships.

She held fate and people responsible. Grumbling, lamenting, and complaining became her habits. She grumbled so much that she developed Alzheimer's. If she'd been content, she might not have suffered so much. Alzheimer's takes people down from wherever they are, much lower than their peers and below the bare minimum. It digs a well and buries them so deep they can never get out again.

This time it was different though. The sickness had deeper, more profound effects on her. She grew more tolerant. Perhaps she realized that circumstances could always be worse. She still had more than those who had lost everything, but people only appreciated what they have when they lose it. She was becoming more contemplative, calmer, and kinder. She endured the pain and suffering with greater ease and humility.

Amir arrived home to find his mother praying on the floor. It was noon, and Zahra had lunch ready. The aroma of Ghormeh Sabzi14 filled the house, Amir's favorite dish. He didn't mind staying and eat with his mother. He had a doctor's appointment that afternoon. The day before, he received the test results from the lab, but the technician didn't tell him much.

He went to the hospital in the morning to submit the receipt to the nurse. The receptionist told him to be there at 4:00 pm. The insurance receipt and test results were in the car. He had no housework to do; so he could have lunch with his mother and enjoy the Ghormeh Sabzi.

Amir called Haleh to tell her that he wouldn't have lunch at home. She didn't like Amir staying with his mother, but after recent events she'd become less sensitive. She wanted to go with Amir to the doctor's visit, but he refused, saying that the children shouldn't be left home alone.

[14] Ghormeh sabzi or Khoresht sabzi, is an Iranian herb stew. It is considered the national dish and is very popular in Iran.

Once the old lady finished praying, she turned her head and looked at Amir. They greeted each other. She asked about Haleh and the children. She wanted Amir to bring them all together for the meal. He told he couldn't because of the kids' busy schedule, but promised they'd find an opportunity soon. The old lady told Amir they were having his favorite food for lunch to encourage him to stay. He got up and went to perform ablutions and pray.

After washing up, he noticed his mother praying again. He took a prayer rug from the bag, facing Mecca to join her. His dedication to prayer and fasting had waned over the years, but he decided to revive his past devotion. His focus had shifted towards spirituality and deeper meaning. He now tried to pray on time. There were many missed prayers to make up too.

Amir completed his Zuhr and Asr prayers and then looked at his mother, still immersed in it. She, too, must be catching up on missed prayers. Perhaps as a plea for healing and longevity. Amir raised his hands for the well-being of his family. Once again, he stood to pray the missed Zuhr and Asr prayers.

His mother gathered her rug, and took a seat at the dining table. Amir joined her for the meal. Zahra served the Ghormeh Sabzi and rice in dishes on the table. Amir said they should wait for Shahram , but the old lady said she wasn't sure he'd come home on time. Amir served his mother and himself, and they began to eat. Zahra brought a pitcher of water and joined them with the old lady's permission.

When they finished lunch, Amir helped his mother to her room, drawing the curtains so she could sleep. When the old lady lay on her bed, she began sharing her lifelong sorrows.

From an outsider's perspective, this family appeared to live a relatively comfortable, trouble-free life. However, those acquainted with them knew the many struggles, hardships, and sorrows they had endured. Not only were their challenges no less than those faced by others, but they were often more complex and grueling.

She recalled the problems they had in her marriage and the financial challenges that they'd lived through, eventually establishing a stable life for their family after many years. When they overcame financial struggles, physical ailments and chronic pain emerged. To her, death was an inevitable truth lurking in every home. It seemed to Amir that his mother was spiritually preparing herself for her ultimate journey.

After unburdening herself and feeling somewhat relieved, she drifted off to sleep. Amir covered her with a blanket and left the room. He occupied himself with the television for a couple of hours, then dressed and left the house.

He arrived at the hospital. The doctor hadn't arrived yet. The seats were all full so Amir settled on standing by a wall.

The other day, he passed the time with a newspaper. This time, he decided to buy a family magazine from a newsstand. He then sat on a bench in the hospital garden and began reading. He had about an hour before the doctor arrive. He read through stories, interviews, psychological advice columns, and family counseling articles. An hour later he stood up and saw Dr. Parsa entered the building, wearing a grey suit and carrying a leather bag.

Amir's eyes followed him as he ascended the stairs, expecting another hour of waiting before it was his turn. He thought about returning to the garden but he didn't really feel like it so he slowly made his way up the stairs.

One of the patients rose from their chair when she heard her name. Amir was delighted to finally find a spot to sit. The speakers called for Doctors Parsa’s patients one by one. There were twelve left so there was some more time to read that magazine.

He’d never heard of pancreatic necrosis before. He searched the internet and found some causes, excessive alcohol consumption being the most common in Western countries. He couldn't find any information about the leading cause of this issue in Iran. Alcohol consumption was common in Iran, but no one addressed it openly, since it was considered taboo.

He knew his problem was likely the same. He wasn't addicted to alcohol, but he did drink occasionally. During their weekly garden gatherings, he’d have a few glasses with friends. It was a ritual, a social custom. Whenever the doctor asked him about his alcohol consumption, he’d deny it. It didn't seem right to tell the truth. In any case, it wasn't socially acceptable. His friends praised alcohol's health benefits, mentioning doctors who claimed it helped regulate blood fat. Although he never had his own blood fat tested, he felt like he’d gained weight recently.

Regarding the disease he never heard of before, he felt embarrassed to ask the doctor about it, fearing that it’d reveal his own alcohol consumption.

Finally, the receptionist announced Dr. Parsa's twelve o'clock appointment. Amir stood up and walked to the doctor's room. This time, he didn’t have to wait too long like the last time. It was a good thing he was currently unemployed and not busy with his company, otherwise he wouldn't have had the time.

After the previous patient left, Amir entered the room. The doctor seemed less tired this time, Amir handed over his test results and insurance paperwork.

The doctor glanced at Amir's previous records, reading through his own notes and recalling Amir's issue. Then he started reading the new test results.

"Are you still experiencing pain?"

“Yes, doctor.”

“Hasn't it lessened?”

“No. It's still the same.”

“Your test results show pancreatic necrosis and inflammation. Your blood fat level is high too. I'll prescribe you some medication for your high blood fat and another one for your pancreatic enzyme replacement. I’ll also prescribe a painkiller. Use it whenever you experience pain, but you should be cautious with it.”

“Thank you. What is the cause of this, doctor? Why did this happen?”

“Well, there are many possible causes. You mentioned not consuming alcoholic beverages, right?”

“No. I don't drink.”

“You had gallstones, right? Well, your high blood fat could’ve played a role, as well as those gallstones, which were likely formed due to cholelithiasis. There might’ve been other factors as well, like heredity. You mentioned not having any family history of this?”

“No. We haven't had anything like this in our family before.”

Dr. Parsa glanced at Amir from above his glasses. He nodded, "Well, the specific cause isn't very important right now. Of course, if there’s a particular factor causing this, it should be addressed to prevent worsening. Your gallstones have been removed. Once your blood fat is under control, hopefully—with the medications, you shouldn't have any problems."

Amir wanted to ask whether he should continue or quit his drinking, but the doctor's implied explanations made it clear that he should quit. Another thing he wanted to know was whether his illness would cause additional problems on his upcoming trip.

“Excuse me, doctor. I may want to take steps to emigrate with my family. I wanted to see if there would be any problem?"

“Well, no. Just have your medications with you wherever you are. Make sure you take them in an orderly manner and keep an eye on your condition. Hopefully you won't encounter any issues.

"Where should I get them from?"

“There’s a pharmacy on the same floor of this hospital. The medications aren't rare. You can find them easily. Don't worry.

“Thank you, doctor. Thank you very much.”

“I wrote a series of tests for you. Bring the results with you next time.

“When should I visit again?”

“Make an appointment for two months from now.”

“I appreciate it. I’ll see you then, goodbye doctor.”

“Goodbye to you too.”

The reason for the sickness was exactly what thought. The doctor didn’t say anything, but it was obvious to him. He went to the receptionist and made an appointment for two months later. He had a strange feeling. When a person realizes they have a disease that may accompany them for the rest of their life, they feel hesitation in their life path. He thought to himself that if his condition worsened in a foreign country and he needed surgery, what would happen to his wife and children?

He went downstairs and entered the pharmacy. He handed the prescription to the pharmacist and waited in the corner. After a few minutes, they called him and gave him a small package to take to the cashier. After paying at the cashier and receiving the medications then left.

Dr. Parsa seemed like a good man. Amir had many questions in his mind about his condition and whether it was curable or not. When he was in front of Dr. Parsa though, he'd get nervous and forget all of them. He didn't know another doctor among his friends and relatives to ask his questions.

His English wasn't fluent enough to understand medical content on the internet. Having friends with different abilities was sure a blessing, he thought.

Dr. Parsa appeared to be a respectable man with a good personality. Everyone praised him and considered him one of the best doctors in the city. What better friend could he have? These doctors had good income and extra money to invest in business ventures. It was a promising thought. If they had a close friendship, their families could get together. They'd have a positive influence on the children's ethics, education, and social skills. Surely, the children of doctors were well-educated like himself. Dara and Delara might find better motivation for studying.

You could be successful and prosperous in Iran too. Dr. Parsa was a good example. What was lacking in his life that he'd want to live in another country? Here, he was more valued and respected because they needed him more. Sure, many doctors preferred to leave Iran, feeling that a better future awaited them elsewhere. But those who stayed weren't lacking anything either. They had everything they wanted. They had respect and dignity too.

He really wanted that if he stayed in Iran, his children could be like Dr. Parsa's children and become someone for themselves. Maybe next time, he could invite Dr. Parsa to their garden and start a family relationship.

22

He patted Dlara's head. Her notebook was neatly organized. She'd learned the alphabet well, but he wasn't sure if she could learn to write words and sentences just as well. She couldn't even read and write in her native Persian language yet.

Dara, on her right, busy with his school assignments. He couldn't learn English this quickly either. He worried that they'd face problems adjusting to their new living environment. Eventually, after a few years, they'd be able to adapt to the new conditions.

These worries were natural. After all, migration was a significant change in their lives, and such a big change needed a lot of effort.

He patted them both on the head. They were his whole life. He had a world of hope and dreams for them. If he wasn't sure that moving to Canada would be good for their future, he'd never consider leaving. But something deep inside him was't satisfied with this decision. He didn't know what it was, but whenever he thought about it, doubt would creep in. He tried to explain what was bothering him, but no matter how much he pondered, nothing came to mind.

He took a deep breath and got up from his seat. Staying at home exhausted him. None of his tasks were progressing either. The house hadn't been sold, and there was no news from Mr. Moradi. His court case also reached a dead end. Maybe it was a blessing in disguise. Perhaps selling the house and investing for migration wasn't in his best interest. Maybe it was a risk. This inner ape led him down a thousand paths and eventually trapped him in the end.

The sound of his phone brought him back to reality. He glanced at it; it was Mr. Zareh.

He answered, "Hello, Mr. Zareh. How are you?

"Hello Mr. Hekmat. Are you feeling better?"

"I'm fine, thank you."

"Thank God. I have good news for you. Mr. Ferasat has settled, and the case is closed."

"Really? Did he have a change of heart?"

"I don't think so. I think he found the necklace himself. Otherwise, he wouldn't have let it go."

"Well, whatever the reason,I'm glad it worked out. Those poor people haven't earned a living in a long time. Thank you so much."

"Ah, don't mention it."

After saying goodbye, he tossed away the phone, joyfully went to Haleh and told her all about it. She raised her hands and thanked God. Amir also thanked God and went to his mobile again. He called his assistant. He asked her to gather the team to start work again in the morning.

During the company's closure, they'd probably lost some of their customers. They could recover with advertising. But when the time comes to leave Iran, he'd have to close the company, advertising would be useless. He smiled. He couldn't stand the company being closed for a few days, let alone closing it and leaving his home and life to migrate to another country. Now he couldn't even think about leaving his family and relatives behind.

He woke up early in the morning. He dressed enthusiastically, got in the car, and left home. He arrived at the company earlier than everyone else. It felt gloomy. He opened the windows to let the air in. A thin layer of dust had settled everywhere. He looked out the window. The sun was rising.

The key turned in the lock, and the assistant entered with a box of sweets in her hand. She smiled when she saw her boss and congratulated him for being back there. She noticed the dust on the table, so she went to the kitchen, brought back a towel to wipe the dust.

The other employees arrived one by one, came to the boss's room to congratulate him, gathered around, and laughed and talked. Amir sat behind his desk in his room, listening to their cheerful voices. Making others happy gave him a sense of satisfaction. Perhaps, God had opened a path of his work with the blessings of the happiness he created in people's hearts.

He felt great. He wanted to share his happiness with others. A party and gathering in the garden didn't seem like a bad idea, but something else bothered him. There was no news from Moradi. The house hadn't been sold either. Finding the necklace and reopening the company meant that God wanted him to continue the business. When he thought about all these together, he doubted his decision to leave.

His thoughts were interrupted by his employee’s voice. They hummed quietly. Amir didn't like this silence. The company was busy before. The phones rang a lot and they had regular customers who needed workers daily. He could call them and tell them about reopening the company. He was also thinking about extensive advertisements through newspapers and text messages. But it was too early. It would be better to first solve the situation with Moradi.

He took his phone and found Moradi’s number. He dialed. It was off. He tried again a few minutes later, but it still said "the phone you are calling is switched off."

He got anxious. He hadn't been able to contact the man for a while now. He didn't know any other lawyers for emigration. Amir called Mr. Zareh and asked him to look into the matter.

He felt a little relieved. After all, Zareh was a good lawyer. He put down his phone and pondered. What if Zareh couldn't figure it out either? He couldn't trust the lawyers who advertised on satellite networks. He had to find a trustworthy person. He didn't know Moradi would end up like this. If he acted without investigating again, the outcome would be unpredictable.

23

He unlocked the garden gate and drove in. Haleh and the kids got out of the car. They grabbed their luggage and went inside the building. It was less cold than before, but still not very warm. The poplar buds were opening. Haleh put the pots on the gas stove and started preparing a salad. Amir started lighting up the coals for the barbeque. The chickens were already marinated. He began skewering them when his phone rang.

He asked Dara to take it out of his pocket. It was Shahram. He'd invited both his brothers for dinner that day. Masoud made up an alibi and Shahram hadn't answered the phone. He asked Amir why he'd called. Amir asked him to attend the lunch party that day. He said Dr. Parsa and his family were invited. Shahram didn't show much enthusiasm at first, but said maybe he'll be able to attend.

Amir wanted to introduce his family to Dr. Parsa. He hoped to boost his brothers' spirits by interacting with distinguished members of society. He'd developed a special interest in Dr. Parsa.

After a long period of pain, thanks to quitting drinking and taking prescription drugs, he felt a sense of vitality. He was drawn to Dr. Parsa's calm and stable personality. He really wanted their families to mingle. Even if they emigrated from Iran, they could stay in touch with them. Haleh agreed. She was especially pleased to learn that Dr. Parsa's wife was also a gynecologist and obstetrician. When she realized that Dr. Parsa, like herself, had a daughter and a son, she took it as a good omen.

A few days before, Amir went to the clinic early and waited for Dr. Parsa to arrive. He thanked him for his effective treatment, and insisted on inviting him and his family to their family garden for dinner that week. Dr. Parsa remembered him. Initially, he declined, but Amir went to the clinic the next day and managed to persuade him. He gave Dr. Parsa a piece of paper with his address and phone number written on it, and told him he'd be waiting for them for dinner on Friday. Dr. Parsa reluctantly accepted, on the condition that the invitation would be canceled if his family weren't up to it.

Amir tried to be the best host possible. Haleh prepared two types of rice and stew. They ordered chicken kebabs from a nearby restaurant. Amir was on his way to pick them up when his mobile phone rang. Dr. Parsa and his family were at the area near the garden and needed a more precise address. Amir went to meet them and guide them to the garden.

Haleh welcomed them warmly. The guests sat on the sofas. Haleh was busy serving them fruits and sweets. The dining table was being set when Shahram arrived. He apologized for her late arrival, and began helping the hosts.

After lunch, Amir and doctor Parsa talked about his disease and how long it'll take to fully recover. Dr. Parsa reassured him that sticking to the meds and a good diet would really help prevent new problems. Amir was worried about his mother's health issues and how hard it was for her to walk again after the fall. Dr. Parsa mentioned that it's hard to say anything without examination and suggested bringing her to the clinic. But Amir didn't want his mom to deal with the crowded hospital.

"No problem," Dr. Parsa said, "You know what? My sister's a physiotherapist, maybe she could see her."

Amir and Shahram were happy with the idea. They asked Dr. Parsa to invite his sister over to the garden. Shahram went to bring the old lady, and Dr. Parsa left to pick up his sister. Haleh thought it was a good opportunity to ask the doctor about her sis-in-law's infertility.

Doctor Parsa's sister told her that she can't say anything for sure without looking at test results.

Within an hour, everyone was back in the garden house. Dr. Parsa, and his sister settled the old lady on the bed, and began examining her. They concluded that the old lady's condition wasn't severe. With therapeutic exercises, and hydrotherapy, she'd improve a lot.

Amir, Shahram, and Haleh all thanked the Parsa family. The old lady, pleased with the Parsa family's behavior, asked Dr. Parsa's sister to visit their home for physiotherapy sessions if possible. Initially, she was reluctant, mentioning that she never conducted home visits for patients and only worked at the clinic. But, with the insistence of the family and her brother's approval, she agreed.

An hour later, the Parsa family decided to leave. Arezoo was asleep next to Delara, but they couldn't find Dara and Omid. Dr. Parsa picked up Arzoo, while Amir went to the garden to look for the boys. He found the two sleeping in a corner of the garden. Dara was holding his toy phone.

Amir tried to wake them up, remembering the time they found Dara unconscious at home. He gently woke them up.

Omid yawned as he rubbed his eyes. Dr. Parsa approached him with concern, "Hey son, you don't usually sleep in the afternoon, what's wrong?"

Amir picked up Dara with a smile, "They're tired from playing."

Amir was lost in thought. The deep sleep of both Dara and Omid today was similar to when Dara passed out the other day. The most likely explanation he could think of was that they'd eaten something that caused it. He searched the garden, but couldn't find any traces of drugs. When he asked Dara, he didn't give a clear answer. The boy just lay back on the sofa with rosy cheeks.

Dr. Parsa thought about Dara's fainting and hospitalization without any apparent cause. The pediatricians had suggested the possibility of poisoning. If the cause of the children's deep sleep today was similar to Dara's fainting, it was possible they had ingested a sedative. Dr. Parsa glanced at Omid,

"Omid, how are you son? Are you okay?"

"I'm fine," the boy replied.

"Are you in any pain? Does your head hurt?"

"No. Why?"

"You were asleep, Omid. Were you tired? Were you playing together?"

"Yeah, we played a lot and danced a lot together. We got tired and fell asleep. But before that, we had something fun!"

"What did you have? What did it look and smell like?"

"It didn't have a smell. It was like water."

"Then you fell asleep?"

"Yeah, after we danced, Dara said we'd feel really good, and then we fell asleep."

"How much did you have?”

"We had it a few times, maybe half. I don't remember exactly. Dara hid the bottle in their fridge after we had some. He said it was his dad's and he shouldn't find out."

Dr. Parsa's wife glanced at her son's half buzzed face, "I keep telling you we shouldn't hang out with just anyone. See what happened? We don't know this family."

"I saw their place, and they seem well-off. They have a villa and a garden outside the city. Wealthy people do these things more often and casually at home."Dr. Parsa said.

"I don't know, I'm not comfortable with us being around this type of family," his wife replied.

"Alright, it was just this one time. Let's move on."

"Better than something happening to the kid. Omid baby are you feeling Ok? Do you have pain anywhere?" the mother asked.

"I'm fine, why?"

"Don't have that stuff again, Omid. It's not good for you."

"I'll call his dad and tell him to keep an eye on. He mentioned his son passing out one time and they didn't find out why. He must have the habit of drinking away from the kids.

"Should I tell the wife too?"

"No. She doesn't drink herself. The boy learned from his father."

Dr. Parsa now knew what Amir's condition was all about.

24

The doorbell rang. Zahra went to answer. The woman came into the yard and closed the gate. Zahra went to greet her.

"Who is it, Zahra?" the old lady asked.

"It's Marzieh, ma'am."

"Oh please,come in."

"Yes, ma'am."

Marzieh entered the hall and greeted the old lady and immediately asked to start their work. The old lady asked her to first have something to drink and refresh, seeing her so tired.

“We'll start after lunch,” she said. She knew Marzieh came straight from the hospital and was probably hungry.

The old lady asked Zahra to bring a glass of cherry juice.

Marzieh took off her hijab and washed her face.

The old lady asked about Dr. Parsa and his wife when they heard the sound of the gate

"It must be Shahram, good. He's here for lunch."

Marzieh put back her hijab. The old lady asked Zahra to bring her a headscarf. By the time Zahra brought the scarf, Shahram entered the hall. Marzieh put on the scarf and greeted him. He answered with a smile.

They had Kalam Polo15 with Shirazi salad for lunch, which was the old lady's favorite food. Zahra served the old lady and Marzieh. Shahram served himself rice and poured some salad on it. The four of them started eating. Marzieh finished eating before everyone else, but the old lady and Zahra insisted she eat more.

"Let her be. You'll ruin her diet," Shahram said jokingly.

The old lady's eyes sparkled, and a smile appeared on her lips. Marzieh blushed and bit her lower lip.

The old lady, Marzieh, and Zahra finished their meal, but Shahram was still eating eagerly. He wanted to serve himself another plate of food when he realized everyone else had finished.

---

[15] kalam polo is a traditional Persian dish with cabbage and beef.

Shahram thanked Zahra. Marzieh also thanked the old lady and asked to help her clear the table, but the old lady didn't allow it. They helped the old lady sit on the sofa. Zahra started removing the dishes from the table, and cleaning it. Marzieh asked the old lady to start her work on the bed in her room, but she preferred to sit there until her food was digested.

Marzieh sat on a piece of furniture and waited while the old lady asked her to turn on the TV for her. Shahram finished his lunch and joined them. The old lady then asked him to help her lie down on her bed for a few minutes before her physiotherapy session. Shahram helped his mother to her room and returned.

He glanced at Marzieh, watching TV, "Isn't it hard for you to work both in the morning and in the afternoon? Two shifts?"

"Life has expenses, what can you do? It's unavoidable." Marzieh replied with a smile.

"I understand, but how much expenses could a single lady have? I'm sure your income is decent."

"Do you think single people don't have expenses? Don't you have expenses yourself?"

Shahram couldn't help but smile and nod in agreement. "True, single people have expenses too. Do you like your job?"

"Yes, thank God. It feels great when you see that you can solve a patient's problems without medication or surgery. Physiotherapy is a rewarding profession."

"Interesting. Good luck with your work."

"Thank you. What about you, are you satisfied with your job?"

"Well, I can't say that I am, but it's not bad either. I work in the stock market."

"That's interesting. I've heard that it can be good if you know what you're doing, but most of it is just a bubble, isn't it?"

"Yes, that's true. The experts say that you should only invest money in the stock market that you don't need. It shouldn't be your main source of income."

"So what is your main source of income then?"

"Uh— it's kind of just this."

"But you said yourself that the stock market shouldn't be your main source of income, so why is it for you?"

"I'm actually an agricultural engineer by degree."

"Oh, that's a field where you should be able to find good work as a man."

"Not really. It's tough finding a good job. It's not as good as you might think."

"Aren't you thinking about finding another job?"

"I am. Do you have any leads?"

"I don't have any leads, but I think it'd be better for you to find a different job."

"Yeah, I'm considering it. God willing, I'll find something better soon."

Marzieh glanced at her watch and stood up. "Well, with your permission, I'll get back to work with your mother."

"Please, go ahead. Thank you."

Marzieh went to the old lady's room. Shahram was left alone on the couch, deep in thought. He knew Marzieh was right. He had to find a stable and fulfilling job. He wanted to get married and start a family, and he needed to have answers for his future spouse. He wanted to show that he could be a reliable and strong husband to share a life with.

Options came to his mind, from starting his own business to working contract-based jobs for government companies. But none of them were suitable for him. He didn't want to have a job that could be done with just a diploma. He wanted to find a job that needed both expertise and was profitable.

Zahra came with a plate of fruit and a few dishes and knives. She placed them on the coffee table in the middle of the hall and went back to the kitchen. She brought a flask of tea, a tray, and a sugar bowl.

"Would you like me to pour you some tea?" She asked.

"No, thank you. I'll have some later."

"Then please, have some fruit."

"Alright. Thank you."

Zahra went to check on the old lady to see if she needed any help. Marzieh was busy with her work, and the old lady was resting comfortably on the bed, a satisfied smile on her lips. Over the past few days that Marzieh had been coming to their home for physiotherapy, not only did the old lady felt less pain, but her spirits also lifted. The previous physiotherapists had done less work for more money. Marzieh, on the other hand, was more efficient, spent more time with her patient, and didn't charge much. They always paid her what she deserved. In any case, the old lady wouldn't allow her to leave unhappy. She liked her strong work ethic and determination. She was fond of her, as if she were her own daughter.

When Marzieh finished her work, she bid farewell to the old lady and left the room. At the insistence of Zahra and the old lady, she sat in the hall to have tea and fruit.

When she finished her tea, she glanced at her watch.

"Are you late? Is your workplace nearby?" Shahram asked.

"It's not very close, but I can manage," Marzieh replied.

Shahram got up, took his car keys, and went to the yard.

"Are you going somewhere?"

"Yes. I want to learn the address of your workplace. One of my friends needs treatment too. Is that okay?"

"Sure. It's fine," Marzieh replied.

They got into the car and set off. Along the way, he said thank you for her dedication to treating his mother. He explained the challenges they faced following his father's passing and how his mother's recent struggle made him appreciate her more while making him realize his own loneliness. His older, married brothers had their own households, and living in a large house with only an elderly parent was difficult.

Marzieh listened silently to Shahram's words, occasionally nodding in agreement. When they arrived at her workplace, Shahram parked the car alongside the street. Marzieh thanked him for the ride.

She got out of the car, and turned to Shahram, "You're not the only one struggling with loneliness."

Shahram's eyes met hers, "May I have your phone number? For when my mother needs an emergency treatment, I'd like to be able to contact you."

Marzieh gave him her number. They said goodbye, and Marzieh entered the clinic.

25

He opened the company door and entered. The receptionist and employees stood up and saluted him. He went to his room, put his bag on the table and hung his coat. He took a deep breath and sat down, then opened his briefcase. There were letters and legal forms for employees that had to be signed. Somebody knocked on the door.

"Come in" Amir said, and the door opened.

One of the workers entered with a box of sweets and an envelope. She opened the box and offered it.

"Okay. What is the occasion?" Amir said with a smile.

"It's my daughter's wedding, sir."

"Congratulations. When will it be Inshallah?"

"The end of this week, God willing," he handed an invitation to Amir, "we'll be honored if you could come, sir."

He took the envelope, "I'd be happy to."

“That’s wonderful sir. You’re always so good to us. We welcome you like a father.”

“Let’s see what happens.”

“We’ll be expecting you. It’s only one night in a poor woman’s house.”

“I do want to come, but Thursdays is for the family. I won’t promise you.”

The woman shook her head "Anyway you see fit. I’ll take my leave.”

”I wish them a happy marriage.”

“With your blessing, Haj Agha.”

The worker took the box of sweets and left the room. Amir opened the envelope and looked at the invitation card. It was a beautiful, unlike any he’d seen before. He placed the card back in the envelope and set it on the desk. He thought for a moment, wishing he could attend the ceremony. Seeing other people’s happiness brought him positive energy, but he knew Haleh wouldn’t attend a stranger's ceremony.

He opened his bag, placed the invitation card inside, and took out his checkbook. He wrote an amount on one of the checks, tore it off, and took it to the worker. He handed her the check, "This is our gift for the bride and groom. Please give them our congratulations."

The worker happily took the check, "Your presence means everything to us. We’re grateful for your kindness."

"Thank you," Amir said. "May they have a blessed life."

The worker took the check, glanced at the amount, and prayed, "May you never face any hardships in life."

Amir smiled and returned to his room. If he had any blessings in life, it was these sincere prayers. And if the company could successfully reopen, it would be thanks to the hopeful eyes of these hardworking employees, a source of income for their daily lives. He was merely a vessel, and it was God who guided their actions. He, too, needed to rely on God to unravel the knots of his own life.

Amir's thoughts shifted to his own problems. His house hadn't been sold, and there was no news from Mr. Moradi. Mr. Zareh hadn't found a good lawyer either. Maybe it wasn't his destiny to leave Iran. With a heavy heart, he took out his cell phone and dialed Mr. Zareh's number.

"Hello, Mr. Hekmat. How are you?"

"Thank you. How are you?"

"Fine, sir. Please, is there anything I can do for you?"

"Any news? Were you able to find a lawyer? Have you forgotten?"

"No, I haven't forgotten, but I'm ashamed to say that I haven't found anyone yet. But let me tell you something interesting."

"What is it?"

"You know Mr. Moradi— you asked me to look for him, right?"

"Yes. What's happened? Have you found him?"

"No, but I investigated and found out that he's a fraud. He's collected thousands of dollars from people promising to get them residency and help them migrate. He cheated everyone and run away. The Interpol is after him. He didn't take any money from you, did he?"

"No, I couldn't collect the money to give to him. He really was a fraud?"

"Never mind that. The bottom line is you were lucky. Thank God you didn't lose anything."

"Thank God indeed. Thanks for following up and letting me know. But you haven't found a lawyer yet?"

"No, I'm sorry. But I'm still looking. If I find a suitable one, I'll let you know for sure."

"Alright, thank you. I was really shocked to hear this news. You mean he really wanted to deceive me too?"

"Didn't he deceive the others? You were no exception."

"That's true. I have to be more careful in the future."

"Be very careful. Don't give your money to just anyone easily. The world has become a pitiful place, full of frauds."

"You're right. I was naive and trusted him too easily. God bless you. Please inform me if you find a reliable lawyer."

"Of course."

"Thank you so much."

"You're welcome. It's my duty."

He was flabbergasted. He couldn't imagine what would've happened if he'd sold his house and given the money to that man. God had truly shown mercy on him by preventing the sale of his house. He'd been through so much suffering in the hospital, narrowly escaping severe consequences of his pancreatic inflammation, as his doctor had warned. Thankfully, his illness passed without any further complications.

Both his mother's hospitalization and Dara's illness had passed without serious consequences.

He discovered Dara's hidden alcohol drinking. He realized that he was primarily responsible for this situation. By keeping and drinking alcohol at home, he'd unknowingly set a bad example for his son.

Amir decided that he'd abstain from alcohol to prevent further harm.

Amir felt immense shame when Dr. Parsa uncovered the issue about the kids drinking. The doctor told him about the long-term effects on the child's mental abilities, leaving Amir with a deep sense of regret. It hadn't occurred to him that if they moved to Canada, it would be difficult to distance themselves from such influences.

He reflected on the failed house sale. It was ultimately for the best. Deep down, he cherished his company and work. During the period the company was closed, he realized how much he depended on it. He wouldn't trade even the challenges for anything else. He was deeply connected to his home, lifestyle, city, and family. He couldn't endure the distress of his mother's illness and his brothers' discomfort. If anything happened to them while he was far away, he'd be unable to do anything.

It dawned on Amir that if he worked hard and persevered here, even the smallest benefits would reach him and his loved ones. In other countries, no matter how hard he worked, his efforts would ultimately benefit others, and he'd remain an outsider. If he could light just one candle here, he knew its light would, however faintly, touch those connected to him. If everyone in a society lit a candle, together they could create illumination for all.

Amir felt a sense of growth within himself. Not only was he responsible for himself and his family, but he also felt accountable to his relatives and community. He was ashamed that he had previously focused solely on his own needs and interests. He remembered when he had first earned his diploma and felt discouraged after being rejected in the national entrance exam. His mother had offered encouragement, saying, "You're still young and God is generous. Try again."

He was grateful to God for his health, strength to fight and persevere, and the opportunity to pursue his desires. He always felt God's presence, no matter where he was. Glancing at his mobile phone, Amir picked it up and dialed Mr. Zareh's number.

She checked her watch. She was a bit early, but she liked being punctual. Entering the park, she enjoyed a stroll among the trees, savoring the spring air and the scent of orange blossoms. This was why they'd chosen this park, even though Shahram preferred the indoors. When she reached the central pool, she walked around it a few times before settling on a nearby bench. She adjusted her scarf, straightened her white coat, took off her sunglasses, and put them on her head. She checked her bag for her phone, but there were no new messages or calls. Another glance at her watch confirmed she was still quite early. She opened a mobile game to pass the time.

After a few minutes, she caught a whiff of masculine cologne. She realized it was Shahram, and looked up to see him standing over her with a smile. She stood to greet him.

"Punctuality isn't exactly your strong suit, is it?" she teased, nodding to his phone. "Buried in your phone, playing games. You could've missed me entirely."

"Sorry," he said. "You were late, so I had to keep myself busy somehow."

"Late? Me? You're delusional."

"Of course, a man is always right. Didn't you know?" he joked.

"Absolutely," she said, playing along. "So, what's this urgent matter you had to discuss?"

"Me? I thought you had something to say. You were the one who wanted to meet," she said.

"Well, I assumed you must've had something on your mind. Thought I'd give you the chance to share."

Marzieh smiled, "You boys are so sure of yourselves."

He laughed, "Anyway, how's work been treating you? Everything okay?"

"Not bad. Could be worse. And you?"

"Not too shabby, thanks be to God. Have you thought about starting your own business?"

"I've considered it, but it's a matter of funding right now."

"What if you had an investor? Would you be open to a partnership?"

"Depends on who the person is and what their terms are. How would it work?"

"The capital would be theirs, but the profit would be split 50/50. Fair enough?" she proposed.

"Seems alright. I'd need to think it over. Who's this investor? Are they trustworthy? Why do they want to do this?"

"They stand to profit too, don't they?"

"True. Are they a friend of yours? Do you know them well?"

"Not a close friend, but I know them. You could get to know them too. We could talk things over, set our terms."

"You know them. You could set terms with them if you want."

"Wait... who is this? You're not... it's not you, is it?"

"Could you really ask for a better partner?" he said, a sparkle in his eye.

"I'm not against it, but are you sure you want this?" she asked.

"If I wasn't, I wouldn't have suggested it. I'm in it for myself too. We'll draw up a solid contract and start on firm footing."

"Thank you. It's a generous offer, and I appreciate your trust in me. I had a proposal for you too, though it's not as good as yours—"

"What's your proposal?"

"A friend's husband has gotten into the import business. Says there's good profit in it."

"Importing what?"

"I'm not sure exactly. Agricultural raw materials and some seeds—I don't know the details. But his field isn't agriculture, so I thought it might be good to partner with someone who has a degree in agriculture. He says the more you invest, the more you earn."

"That's how it works in any business. More investment, more profit."

"My friend said her husband is looking for an investor. I thought you might want to consider it."

"Not a bad idea. I'll think about it. The important thing is that he's trustworthy. How well do you know him? Do you trust him?"

"I've known my friend for a long time, but I can't really vouch for her husband. You're right, trustworthiness is key. You could get to know him better, talk to him, then decide."

"Right now, I don't have much money. But we can start this partnership, and when I have some more, I can invest in other businesses too. Are you open to partnering with them?"

"I don't have a lot of money either, but if I did, I would consider it."

"So you don't distrust them?"

"No. I said they're not bad people. His wife is my friend."

"Good. We'll think about it when the time comes. For now, let's focus on our own investment. Agreed?"

"Very good."

"First, you should consult with your family and anyone else you'd like. We'll draft a contract with a lawyer present. Then you give me a list of what we need and look for workers while I buy the equipment. Can you find workers?"

"Yes, no problem. My plan is ready. My friends are at university and can help."

"So it's all set. Consult with whomever you need and let me know."

"Won't you consult with your family? Your older brothers? Your mother?"

"There's no need. My brothers and I don't interfere in each other's work. As for my mother—"

"What about her?"

"She's never cared about these things, and she has her own health issues to worry about now. She's been awake for some time, I told you before."

"After my father passed—"

"May God have mercy on him."

"May God have mercy on those you've lost too. After he passed, my mother was never the same. Day by day, she grew sicker, angrier. Her Alzheimer's and depression came first, then leg weakness and—you know the rest. "

"May God grant her healing quickly."

"Healing is in God's hands. As for me— I have only my brother, who lives with me. He'll help me decide, but he won't pressure me. His opinion matters to me."

"So you'll consult with him?"

"Of course. He's very experienced."

"You're lucky to have such a brother. Cherish him."

"You have a good family too, kind and upstanding. Know their worth."

"That's good of you. See us as your own family. My mother considers you like the daughter she never had."

"Speaking of daughters, what's the story with the daughter your father could have had?"

"How did you hear about that? Did Zahra tell you?"

"Never mind, someone mentioned it."

"I— don't know what to say. My father's daughter is from his first marriage, but we don't see her."

"Why not? Did something happen?"

"I'll explain when there's a better time."

"Alright, whatever you're comfortable with."

Shahram stood up, brushing off his pants. "We've talked too much. Don't you feel thirsty? Wait I'll be right back."

Without waiting for Marzieh's response, he left. Moments later, he returned with two Ice creams. Marzieh said thanks.

The park lights turned on, and the fountain in the middle of the pool began to work. A cool breeze blew around them. The park guard was pacing among the trees, watching them from afar.

While eating the ice creams, Marzieh explained what they needed for a physiotherapy clinic and how they could improve their work and attract more clients. They agreed that Shahram would visit Marzieh's workplace at the hospital and clinic to better understand their working conditions.

The ice cream was melting. It dripped onto their clothes. Shahram noticed a stain on his pants. He said a loud Ah and put the rest of it in his mouth. Marzieh looked at her ice cream; her clothes were also stained. She gasped and tried to get a handkerchief out of her pocket. She found it, cleaned herself. They both chuckled.

The park guard arrived. He gave them a stern look and pointed to the families sitting around, "This is a place for families. You two behave, alright?"

Shahram looked back at the guard uncomfortably, "What did we do?"

“I told you, this isn't the place for these kinds of games.”

Shahram got up angrily to confront the gurad, but Marzieh stopped him.

“It’s Ok. We were just leaving. Come on, let’s go,” She said.

"You didn't let me teach him a lesson," Shahram said.

"It's not worth getting involved with these kinds of people. Let's just forget it. We've finished our work anyway."

"I said let's go to a more comfortable coffee shop. You said no, you prefer the park."

"Parks have their own rules. Now let's just leave."

"I'm not coming to the park again."

"Fine, we won't come to the park again."

"Next time we'll go to a coffee shop. Actually, why a coffee shop? Let's go to my place, sit, talk. It's not like we're going to do anything."

Marzieh laughed, "Alright, whatever you're comfortable."

He got out of the car, opened the door, and entered the courtyard. When he entered the hall, the old lady was sitting alone on the sofa. He carried the nylon bag to the kitchen. He took out packages of meat and put them in the freezer, and told his mother that Zahra would cut them into pieces and cook them tomorrow. He asked about Shahram. His mother told him he was asleep in his room. Amir went to Shahram's room, pushed him aside, "What kind of man sleeps until noon?"

“Leave me alone. It’s Friday.”

“It's Friday, so what? Don't you want to give me a hand?”

“Alright, I'm coming. You should’ve told me earlier.”

“Now that I'm here, get up, let's take mother and go.”

“You go, we'll come later.”

"Don't make me pour a bowl of ice water on you," he pushed the blanket aside, "Get up already."

Shahram sat up and rubbed his eyes. He yawned and glared at Amir with sleepy eyes.

“Well, if you’d called, I would’ve brought mother, and we would’ve come. You didn't need to come yourself.”

“I had something to do, I had to come home.”

“What?”

I brought a few packets of Nazri16 meat and put them in the freezer. Tell Zahra to cook them tomorrow.

---

16 In Islam, the word nazr (Arabic: نذر) is a vow or commitment to carry out an act. When it works out people usually feed the poor.

“You should’ve given half of it to that same welfare center.”

“Yes, I'm aware. I'm going now. You get mother and come to the garden. Everyone is there. Come quickly and help me with the kebabs.”

Shahram got out of bed, "By the time you get there, we'll be there too. Do you need anything from home? A tablecloth, utensils, fruit or sweets or something?"

“No, I've bought everything. Just get yourself there quickly. We have a lot of work to do.”

He left Shahram's room and told his mother all those instructions as well. He got into his car and set off. He’d been feeling intense pain since morning. While driving, his pain intensified. He felt nauseous and feverish. He hadn't taken his medication for a few days. He couldn't accept being dependent on pills for a lifetime. No matter how hard he tried not to show the pain and ignore it, he couldn't bear it. He was forced to park on the side of the road. He pressed his hands against his stomach and vomited.

He wanted to go to the hospital, but how could he leave his guests at the garden party? He took his medication from the dashboard and swallowed a few pills. He decided to stop there for a few minutes until the pain subsided. Ten minutes passed, but the pain didn't change. The agony took away his ability to move. Even in this state, he couldn't accept being unresponsive to his guests.

With difficulty, he turned on the car and moved. When he arrived at the hospital, he parked his car and went to the emergency room. The emergency doctor asked him to describe his condition and examined him. He requested several tests. He asked the doctor for painkillers. The doctor prescribed them but asked him to wait for the test results under observation in the emergency room.

Amir went to the laboratory. Vials of blood were taken from him. Then he went to the pharmacy to get his medication. Then, he sat on the chairs in front of the lab, waiting for the test results. His eyes fell on the clock inside the hall. It was almost lunchtime, but he still hadn't prepared the kebabs. He took out his phone and called Shahram. He told him he might be late. Shahram wanted to know the reason. Amir said that one of his friends had gotten sick, and he had to go to the hospital.

His anxiety eased a bit. He understood the value of his brother and loved ones better in these conditions. He remembered his only sister. They hadn't heard from each other in a long time. He missed her. He wished he'd invited her to the party as well. He had her number on his mobile. They occasionally asked each other how they were doing. But now, it was too late to invite her. She probably wouldn't come for lunch, but she could come for dinner. At least he could ask how she was doing.

He picked up his phone and dialed her number. She asked about Haleh and the children. Amir asked about her husband and sons. He told her about his own and his mother's surgeries. Nasrin wanted to come to the hospital to visit him. Amir reassured her it was a few months ago, but he invited her to the garden for lunch. Nasrin apologized and said she needed to attend to her children. He asked her to join them for dinner, but she declined. They talked for a few more minutes and said goodbye with wishes for health and happiness for themselves and their families.

He couldn't describe all that happened in a few minutes, and he didn't see the need for it either. He put his phone in his pocket and looked at the laboratory door. The test results would be ready in a few more minutes. He felt his pain had subsided a bit, but it was still bothering him. He got up from his seat and walked a little.

A few minutes later, he went to the laboratory door. He received the test results and went to the doctor's office. The orthopedic doctor looked at the test results and shook his head, "The results are not bad, but they're not completely normal either. An internist should also examine you."

“Where can I find an internist on a holiday?”

Don't worry. We have an internist here. I'll write a referral for you. Stay in the orthopedics department. We will contact them and inform them about your condition. How is your pain now? Are you feeling better?”

“I'm not too bad, but I still have pain. Doctor, can I go home now? I have a lot of guests for lunch today. They're waiting for me.”

“I'm saying this for your own good. You have chronic pancreatitis. It's possible that acute inflammation has also occurred. If it gets worse, it can be very dangerous. First, make sure you don't have any serious problems, then you can go home.”

“When is your doctor coming?”

“Stay under observation for a few hours first. Then we'll decide whether to hospitalize you or discharge you based on their assessment.”

“So, I have to be here for at least a few hours?”

“Yes, unfortunately. It's better this way.”

It seemed he had no other choice. He took the prescription and, after thanking the pharmacist, went to the orthopedics department. He got the medicines and gave them to the nurses.

The nurses asked him to have a companion to take care of him, but he didn't want anyone involved in this problem. He hoped that he'd no serious issues and would be discharged soon.

He lay on the bed, his arm connected to an IV administering medication when his mobile phone rang. Haleh wanted to know where he was. He had to come up with a series of lies about his friend's emergency hospital visit. Haleh told him everyone was already there. Amir, caught in his lies, told her that he couldn't make it to lunch. He asked her to keep the guests busy. He promised to explain the whole situation to her as soon as possible. Haleh wasn't happy about it with all those guests and her husband being absent.

They'd organized a big party, and close family members were going to stay until late at night. Haleh suggested that Amir ask Dr. Parsa for advice, but he said it wouldn't be right for that poor man to leave his party because of their problem.

After a few hours of hospitalization and receiving painkillers, Amir's pain subsided. The internal specialist came to the hospital. He examined Amir and made him promise to take his medications on time, he was granted discharge permission. Amir happily paid the bill and returned to the party.

When he arrived at the garden, it was already afternoon. Most of the guests had left, leaving only Haleh's sisters, Shohreh, and her mother. Dr. Parsa's family and sister had stayed for dinner at Shahram and Haleh's request. The aroma of the stew filled the entire garden. When he arrived there, he told them about the incident.

"You were probably careless. You should eat less fatty food, "Said Dr. Parsa.

"No, doctor," Amir replied. "I'd forgotten to take my medication for a few days."

"I hope you won't forget again."

The sky was growing dark. They watered the garden and sat on a large rug, talking. As usual, Amir's brother-in-law brought his Hafez poetry book from his car and read a few poems. Taking omens was a tradition of theirs. Whoever wanted, would make a wish and they'd open the Hafez book randomly and read a poem as a sign. Some would laugh, while others would drown deep in thought.

Amir asked for his own fortune to be read. They handed him his Hafez book so he could open it himself. Amir closed his eyes, recited the opening chapter of the Quran, and made a wish.

He placed his finger on a random page opened it. It was a strangely befitting line. He read it for everyone to hear;

Turbid be the wine or clear, drink merrily

For all is a blessing from our heavenly patron

www.ingramcontent.com/pod-product-compliance
Lightning Source LLC
LaVergne TN
LVHW010354160826
845677LV00005BA/1271

* 9 7 9 8 8 9 2 9 8 7 8 4 4 *